I'M OLD, I'M WISE, & I KNOW MY SH*T

Bevinda Collaço has been a print and online journalist, agony aunt, visiting postgraduate lecturer and media person for more than forty years. She has two measly death threats to her credit, but lots of God's blessings. She became a grandmother in 2016 and recognised a need to write this book for women of any age. She lives in Goa, India.

I'M OLD, I'M WISE, & I KNOW MY SH*T

FOR THE WOMAN WITHOUT A PLAN
AND THE MAN WITHOUT A CLUE

BEVINDA COLLAÇO

An imprint of Manjul Publishing House Pvt. Ltd.
• C-16, Sector 3, Noida, Uttar Pradesh 201301, India
Website: www.manjulindia.com
Registered Office:
• 10, Nishat Colony, Bhopal 462 003 – India
Distribution Centres
Ahmedabad, Bengaluru, Bhopal, Kolkata, Chennai,
Hyderabad, Mumbai, New Delhi, Pune

Bevinda Collaço asserts the moral right to be
identified as the author of this work

ISBN 978-93-90924-76-9

This edition first published in 2021

Cover Design: Sasitha Ramanathan

In memory of
Sharon and Wendell,
who nagged me to write this book and then died
one after the other without so much as a by-your-leave.

Contents

Part III
Notice How Family Begins With an F?

Part IV
Fly Over That Hill

Author's Note

This book has been burning holes in me for twenty years thanks to a 'temporary' agony-aunt column dumped on me as part of my duties as a journalist. I did it, not because I believed that liar of an editor when he said it was temporary, but because desperate people were asking for help. Most needed advice. Many needed actual physical help. But all needed someone to tell them that theirs was a mistake anyone could have made.

I ran that temporary agony-aunt column for seven years and, judging by the slew of letters invoking God's blessings on me, even by readers who had not written in with their personal crises, my solutions worked. The problems were common to so many.

At my end was a broken defeated victim. At the other end was one poor decision caused by desperate love for an unworthy piece of crap, followed by a domino effect of more poor decisions. The piece of crap was a partner, neighbour or child. Sometimes a monster who had no business being a parent. Sometimes a boss.

I am not too sure if it is a good thing or not, but I attract personal secrets from all sorts of people. I heard victims, abusers, friends and relatives. I read and randomly chatted up mental-health professionals for solutions.

Their words convinced me that desperate love for anything or anyone usually gets you fucked. If you don't recognise it as an addiction, desperate love will drag you down and destroy you.

Mine were not politically correct solutions, and sure enough mental-health professionals began objecting. So I would consult them on dealing with peer pressure, falling desperately in love, teen fears about first-time sexual intercourse, marriage, parenting, mental abuse, domestic violence, dealing with a break-up, empty-nest syndrome, midlife crisis, menopause and the dread of being invisible in old age. These were the contents of the letters that landed on my desk. And they became the blueprint for this book.

These were common problems back in those agony-aunt crusade days decades ago, and you know what? They are common problems today, decades later. Too many women are wired to sweep their personal needs under the carpet—whether it is career, companionship or sex.

There's another problem.

No one raises a word against the gender-brainwashing women are hammered with since birth. I don't profess to be the first or last to call this out and to urge women to take back our space. Like so many others, I am one more voice with the weight of experience behind me. You cannot have too many voices telling women, hey, it's okay to call out bullshit when you see it.

You will therefore find four parts in this book. Part 1 is about setting up a Bullshit Radar for teens to twenties to recognise early signs of a potentially rotten relationship before it bites them in the ass. It's about distancing from the wrong people. There's a chapter on the joy of sex, which talks of the usually underwhelming experience of one's sexual debut.

Part 2 is about handling the pain of disrespect, mental abuse, domestic violence, divorce and death. There's a Compatibility Questionnaire I'm pretty pleased with and the four elements that make for lasting happiness.

Part 3 is a factual look at how childbearing and parenting is not meant for everyone. They swallow the best years of your life because that's when shit gets real.

Part 4 is a fun ride for handling the fifty-plus tripwires of empty-nest syndrome, midlife crisis, menopause and workable ideas for turning this last lap into the best time of your life—also putting the 'fun' into funeral by planning your own.

In these decades that have sped by like you wouldn't believe, I learnt one truth: never commit to anyone or anything to the exclusion of all else. Don't tell me about stars in your eyes and ants in your pants. Whether young or old, you should know that stars in your eyes won't let you see clearly and ants in your pants will bite.

I wish my schoolmates and I had this book in our high school compulsory reading list. We knew nothing.

I am writing this book for teenagers, for women of any age about to enter into a serious relationship. Most specifically, however, I am writing this book for young mothers. The solution lies in their hands. Hopefully they can use this to gain some additional perspective on raising their daughters to deal with the suckiness of life. I'm hoping, also, that they can make plans for not turning invisible in their old age. Old age is our last lap;

if we don't make it count, what's the point of merely existing?

This is also a handy ready-reckoner for men who don't have a clue about women. This book is about cisgender women and navigating heterosexual relationships, but one of my closest friends who is proudly homosexual, says this book is a blueprint for any relationship and any individual, straight or LGBTQ.

The one thing that does not change is the quality of a relationship between two individuals. Another thing that does not change is the solid core of loving and respecting oneself first, regardless of gender or orientation. Cautionary: I am not a preachy person, but there may be statements that sound preachy. It happens when you are almost as old as the hills and you *know* your shit. Still, if you find such preachiness, I do beg your pardon. Feel free to ignore it; focus instead on the message.

Part I

Survival Smarts for Teens and Twenties

1

Bullshit Radar—The Teen Weapon for Peer and Social Pressure

Adolescence is a horrible time of life, see-sawing between the awesome confidence of childhood and the extreme self-doubt of stepping into the adult world. Teens feel the need to fit in, as do adults. Nothing wrong with that except when the need to fit in gets desperate, you make poor decisions. And then there are the lies...

I expect she's sizzling in hell, but the nun who taught us Catechism scared the shit out of us at the age of seven. I mention this incident to prove my point that the crazy lies begin way before adolescence. What made the nun really scary was that she began her story with the sweetest expression on her face when she described our souls to us. Stained at birth with just one Original Sin, our souls were washed dazzling white with Baptism, is what she told us.

After that she informed us that every time we sinned, we left a pus-oozing sore on that pure white soul that turned grey and rotten whenever we stepped off the straight and narrow. Our souls were a gift from God she said and suddenly looked at us with the coldest reptilian eyes. Did we want to give Him pus-ridden, sin-infused rotten souls? Did we? DID WE? She leaned forward on her desk, elbows up, peering into each pair of wide eyes like an iguana up to no good at all.

We were terrified. But human weakness prevailed and some years later, at the age of thirteen, I have a very clear memory of a classmate who ignored the nun. She matured earlier than the rest of us in terms of acquiring boyfriends.

One day on the school playground, she placed her problem squarely before a group of us. She was sure she was pregnant because her boyfriend touched his tongue to hers.

Opinion was divided since none of us had a clue about the process of impregnation. Some were doubtful; other voices of doom were certain that she could get pregnant. Almost all of us thought saliva was gross, but she assured us it was an essential ingredient for making a baby. That was the level of our knowledge when we were in our early teens.

Today's thirteen-year-olds have more access to these ticklish questions than we did, but despite today's information overload they are still as much in the dark as we were.

If you are the parent of a teen, the first thing you learn is teens like fighting the family and fitting in with peers, who may or may not be their friends. Many troubled teens have crossed my path, and without exception they agree that what they need is a working Bullshit Radar to help them suss out the bullshit that is presented to them daily.

The Bullshit Radar comes in handy through life, and it's a survival kit that is simple to set up. It's the common-sense approach to life situations and people.

Once we are in our teens, not only are our boobs and bristly body hair growing, our minds are growing too. Our old points of view are challenged and we begin tweaking our thinking, unlearning what we learned.

Thinking for oneself is cool. Proper cool is getting more information to figure out which ideas and challenges will work for us. And which ones will end up with egg on our faces.

Girls have been wired from birth to give huge props to romantic relationships and the mutual 'I love you'. No one tells us that the mutual 'I love you' is not the end of the story. The story could go bad six months later. But all the love stories and all the films, even detective thrillers and hospital thrillers, have the 'I love you' as the high point of the story. No one warns you that if you allow it, a bad relationship can permanently mess up the quality of your life like you wouldn't believe.

Society expects women to be weak and yielding when it comes to relationships, but they want them to have Incredible Hulk-type strength when it comes to working for others. Then Life barrels up and shows us that weak and yielding get us nowhere.

They never tell us that if you are female and a teen or a thirty-year-old or a hundred-year-old, you have to be secure in your own mental and physical space. They never tell us that we must understand and be comfortable with who we are and where we want to go. You can tell yourself all this and more when your Bullshit Radar is fully functional.

All a BS Radar needs for installation in our minds is just this: If you hear something that is too good to be true, accept that it is probably a lie. If you hear someone demanding great sacrifice from you, ask yourself first if that sacrifice will make you happier in the long run.

If there is a doubt in your mind, follow it through and ask the question to clear that doubt. Briefly the Bullshit Radar is this:

- When what you hear sounds too good to be true, pay close attention
- When what you hear sounds too painful a sacrifice, pay close attention
- Crosscheck what you were told
- Question the speakers
- Hold them accountable

That's it. That's all you need. When you question, you get information, and the other person knows you will not fall for their tall stories. You need to be informed because everybody lies. In itself that's actually a pretty good thing. Imagine the chaos if everyone the world over decided to tell the truth, even for a day. There would be all-out war.

We go through life subconsciously absorbing certain truths, but it takes experts like Pamela Meyer, author of *Liespotting*, (another word for BS Radar) to state the obvious that was in front of us all along. Meyer says everyone lies. We are constantly hit with lies of different kinds.

Sometimes they are white lies that you want to hear ('No, you don't look fat' or 'Oh...your profile pic is so hawt!') and sometimes they are lies that destroy our quality of life ('If he's buying me an expensive meal, it's only fair to give him a blow job,' and before you know it, a video of you and he is going viral). Sometimes the truth is so painful that we lie to others to protect them, or we just don't have the courage to tell it like it is. Often we lie to feel good about ourselves.

It takes two to allow a lie to exist, says Meyer, the liar and the one who chooses to believe that lie. Belief is a choice. And when you choose to believe a lie, you end up feeling like all kinds of a fool.

The BS Radar, on the other hand, signals you to question what you hear, especially when it feels too good to be true. You don't even have to be a full-on detective inspector about it. All you need to do is crosscheck. Go on, take your BS Radar for a trial run and question those fairy tales they read out to us during our childhood.

Why were fairy tales never gifted to our brothers?

Did we ever ask our parents and relatives why fairy tales were not read or gifted to our brothers? They were reserved for girls. The guys received books on travel, science and adventure while we got rainbows and unicorns. Our gender brainwashing began there.

Girls are given rainbows and unicorns as mind-developing materials, when any fool knows that rainbows are a mirage and unicorns are a myth.

Kiss a frog and he turns into a prince? In real life the exact opposite happens. Girl kisses her good-looking prince and a few years later, he turns into a frog. Sometimes he's a nice frog, but most times, he is mean, lazy and overbearing. We select handsome hunks because they make *us* look good. That's great, but along with making you look good, it is important that he makes you *feel* good too. Otherwise, what's the point really?

The BS Radar will tell you to keep those fairy tales, steamy romance paperbacks, porn and novels of selfless love as entertainment, but definitely not as a blueprint for your life. If you want selfless love or a perennial stud and you don't get it, you are going to be feeling seriously cranky a few months into the relationship.

When I was fifteen, I read O. Henry's *Gift of the Magi,* and it shook me to the core. A young, desperately poor couple wanted to get each other a Christmas gift. She had wonderful long, glossy hair and he had this waistcoat watch with a broken chain. He sold his watch to buy pearl combs for her lovely long hair, but she sold her hair to buy a chain for his watch. I wanted that kind of selfless love. Today, however, because I'm old, wise and *know* my shit, I call it typical poor communication between husband and wife.

If you are reading fairy tales to your little girl, encourage her to question them. The world is dumbing down and we need clued-in people to see through the BS. Hansel and Gretel finding that house made of cake in the forest—how come the forest ants didn't find it first and demolish it? Let your little girl get into the habit of seeing something fake and questioning it.

No one ever told us that questioning is a life skill needed for protecting our ass. Instead we are groomed to believe everything we are told and we get taken for a ride, not once, not twice, but time and time again.

Falling for every line you hear is not the end of the world, of course, but there's a whole lot less tension and heartbreak if you question. There's a lot less murder in your heart too, especially when you find yourself forced to do something you don't want to do. You know something is a lie but you have to go along with it just to keep the peace. How often have you been in a situation when to avoid a scene, you said, 'Sure, I'll do it', while your mind was going 'Fuck you!'?

Peer pressure

Who hasn't looked up to a group of cretins and wanted in so badly you could taste it? You want to be part of a group that lives up to your idea of cool. It could be the achiever cool or the dangerous cool. You may be exposed to both kinds of peer pressure: positive or negative. Let's do the good group first.

This good group challenges us and helps us better ourselves, and that's called Positive Peer Pressure. I was briefly part of a group like that, but left it rapidly. The goody two-shoes help us get better grades, better social skills, they get you to stop smoking, to say no to drugs and they will stop you from hooking up with every guy in sight. Which is all good, yes? The downside is that they make you feel less than worthy as you become their on-going Pygmalion project.

The other type of group influence is Negative Peer Pressure. This one ruins the quality of your life and of those around you. A working Bullshit Radar signals negative peer pressure immediately. There are two types of negative peer pressure.

There is the in-your-face continuous series of dares to prove that you 'fit in' with the cool crowd. That's easy to recognise. If you like living dangerously, taking risks and being fearless, you'll be a perfect fit.

It's the other one that is difficult. That one is more sophisticated and is fraught with more long-term difficulties for the unaware teen. In this kind of peer pressure, there are no dumb dares.

They merely present you with what they consider a cool lifestyle. They crown themselves social leaders. They make you feel that it is a privilege to join them, to be associated with them and to be seen with them. This kind of negative peer pressure is more common.

No one dares you to do anything, but if your peers drink alcohol or do drugs, you may feel the need to fit in. If they see nothing wrong with having casual unprotected sex, you may too. If they shoplift, steal and vandalise, you may do the same. If they find cyber bullying highly entertaining, so might you.

We go along with them because we want to be with them. In youth it's called peer pressure; in middle age it's called 'keeping up with the Joneses'. In old age it's called 'ageing gracefully', but the wise ones know that ageing *dis*gracefully is where the joy is.

We ignore what we know to be right and consciously do wrong, just to belong. This, even when we know those actions are hurting us and those close to us.

So what do you do? Join or run for your life?

You know what the group expects of you. You have a pretty

good idea of what your limits are. If you know you can do what they ask of you, you step up to the plate. If you get that rabbit-caught-in-the-headlights feeling, stop and take a long slow breath. If you feel sick and frightened, that's when your Bullshit Radar must kick in. Think the thing through. Focus on the fact that the cool group will not hang around to protect you from the fallout.

It is you who wants to join them; they don't care either way because you may increase their number by one, but they were doing pretty well before you came along. You are a source of amusement for the moment; if you have something they want, they'll take you in. The dares are just entertainment for them and a rite of passage for you.

It's good to know that peer pressure will take up a very short period of your life and will be gone before you know it. Also, it's good to remember that most often the cool kids in school and college peak early. It is easy to strut around in a small group but once they get into the adult world, that strut becomes unsure. They don't make the rules anymore. It is the quiet nerds more often than not who end up calling the shots.

With negative peer pressure, you are made to commit harmful or illegal actions. You can do it, deal with the fallout of video-recorded evidence and hope it does not screw up your future. Or you can refuse to do it.

If you refuse to go along with the dare, expect derision and insult. Expect shaming and shunning. Whatever you do, don't be apologetic about it. Refuse confidently and firmly without showing any fear of rejection by the group, even if you are quaking inside. Never show them that you are vulnerable.

David Maxfield and Joseph Grenny, authors of a number of bestsellers including *Change Anything,* explain why smart people do dumb things when they're simply 'following the crowd'. They say the group will follow the leaders, even while knowing that the action is wrong. The thing to do, they say, is to quietly but firmly express doubt and you will find two-thirds of the group agreeing with you.

I respectfully disagree with Messrs Maxfield & Grenny because I'm old and wise. In every peer pack, there is a leader and his or her sidekicks. They will not give up control easily. Your doubt or refusal to do something they want you to do will be seen as challenging their authority.

There will be pushback, but if you tap into your own set of values, it's easy to repeat a firm refusal. That's called owning your space. You don't need to be a leader or a follower if you are fine on your own. You walk your own path like a boss.

You will always find kindred souls around you. Or they will find you. When you show a disinterest in fitting in, people come into your life and enduring friendships are born.

Society's pressure on women

That BS Radar must alert you into recognising society's unrelenting pressure on us. It begins from the time we can follow simple instructions. Our social engineering into being the perfect princess began with those fairy tales they read to us when we were toddlers. I blame Hans Andersen, Aesop and the brothers Grimm for screwing up the world for women over the centuries.

We grew up from little girls in pigtails with our heads full of handsome princes and palaces and magical happily-ever-afters, to lovely young women reading lurid romance paperbacks that ended with marriage. We so wanted the tall, dark, brooding, broad-shouldered, slim-hipped handsome hero with thick crisp hair and fire in his eyes.

Well, I know something about the tall, dark, brooding, handsome guy with the thick crisp hair and so on. While I am willing to concede that there may be exceptions, all the brooding men I know (and women too for that matter), are really painful to live with in a long-term relationship. Brooding? Their partners tell me that they sulk when they don't get their way and they have no sense of humour. You and I know that one of the best stress busters is to share a laugh over the silliness of the day. If you cannot, then what is the point, really?

Show me one fairy tale that speaks of compatibility between the prince and princess after their fairy-tale marriage. How did they get along after the royal wedding? Did they bicker over which side of the bed they wanted? Did he get cranky because he was up at dawn and she had breakfast at noon? Was he a narcissistic control freak who had no empathy? Were their royal kids royal pains? Did the couple fight over money? Did she want a career? Did he want a night out with the guys every week? No one knows. Did the beautiful princess have fibroids and find sex painful? Did she have PMS mood swings and homicidal temper tantrums? Did their breath smell vile in the mornings? Were they fine with each other's farting and snoring? Show me the fairy tale that speaks of divorce and of who got custody of the young prince and princess. Who got the palace and who had to move out? They never tell us that. Sleeping Beauty marries Prince Charming and they lived happily ever after—full-stop.

Mind you, that's just literature for toddlers. That unreality is embedded in their minds at such an early age. It continues, though. There's so much more for different ages. There's advertising, films, music, literature, theatre, newspapers and magazines, radio and television telling us how we should live our lives.

Watch toddlers playing in front of the television set. They stop what they are doing and focus on the screen when the ads stream. They watch those ads with happy shiny people enjoying a happy shiny life and they form images deep in their subconscious.

They watch mass media play the wife and mother card every chance it gets. Mass media will speak soulfully of the joy of motherhood and of the immense contribution of mothers to the world. Media empires have been built around convincing girls that it is their duty to marry and have children.

From the womb to the tomb, everyone knows that children directly ramp up the profits of Big Business. Who supplies children to big business? Mothers. The daily message beamed into our consciousness is that all that agony of giving birth to and looking after a pack of children is something we should glory in and find validation for ourselves as women. This, your Bullshit Radar will tell you, is a total crock.

Women themselves are to blame. Why would anyone tell their child to marry and deliver babies when she grows up? Like it's so easy? There is a whole chapter in this book dedicated to the horrid truths about pregnancy and a whole other one on the obscenity that is the natural delivery. Women know.

They *know* that not only is motherhood the toughest and most thankless job, they know you cannot retire from it. Still they tell their little daughters that this is a beautiful thing. They groom them with lady dolls and baby dolls and tea sets and doll houses, while their little brothers get the fun things: cars, bikes, planes and guns. Ever wondered why school shooters are always boys or men? That should tell us something, shouldn't it? This sexism from infancy makes me so mad.

No one ever worries that instead of a prince, that little girl could end up with a monster she is expected to forgive for every insult and every assault on her.

Your BS Radar will help you choose what works for you. You could fit your life around hunting for validation from your peers and society. Or you need not. The fact is that while some of us are born to be mothers, not all of us are parent material.

Look at the traumatised children around us, desperate for attention that they need but don't get from their parents. Not all of us are built to be happy and capable in domestic relationships. There are women whose Bullshit Radars showed them that childbearing and rearing were not for them and they said 'No'. There are growing numbers of women and men who prefer freedom from 'domestic bliss'.

Society frowns on them because they committed the sin of Individual Choice. Society is very allergic to individual choice.

2

You Aren't Perfect. So?

Are you second-guessing yourself most of the time because you think you are not good enough? Are you juggling your life around to make time for him all the time? Did you think he was The One but now you find he's really nothing special?

If you listen to interviews of the most beautiful and talented people in the world, you will find them all disparaging something or the other about themselves. So if you think you are physically flawed, overweight, or have a huge nose, or you think you aren't cool enough, or hot enough, or bright enough... All I can tell you is: enough. No one is perfect. Get that? No one. So don't just accept your 'flaws', embrace them.

Perfection by my definition *has* to be boring. You are done. There's nothing more to do. To be flawed is fun because there is always something interesting and out of the ordinary about you. You may be unhappy about some perceived less-than-perfect aspect of you, but it can actually save you tons of grief, like my large chest.

Let me tell you about an epiphany I had recently right after falling flat outside a lingerie store. I'm generally okay with my extra kilos, but get severe tension when I have to buy lingerie. Not any longer though after the recent incident.

Now, on to the story. I enter this lingerie place. The salesgirl eyes my large chest and guesses, 'Uhh... 38? No, Madam, you should try 40.'

I tell her self-righteously that I am wearing size 38, but she gives me a size 40 anyway. I proceed to a changing room and try it on. It's a struggle. I finally fix the clasps and, panting like a long-distance runner, I look in the mirror. The changing-room mirrors mockingly show me my front and my back. The bra is so tight it has given me boobs on my back too. I struggle out of the size 40 straight-jacket and back into my very old, very comfortable but well-fitting only-two-boobs 38 and leave the shop feeling insulted.

I was so annoyed at the unfairness of it all that I did not see the incomplete ramp some jackass left in my path. My toe caught on the edge of it and I was airborne, parallel to the ground. I slammed down with my size 38-maybe-40 boobs to cushion my fall. I must have bounced, because I was up in a flash before anyone could reach me and fled the scene. I checked my vitals and except for a slight soreness on one knee everything was working fine. But hey, those troublesome boobs of mine actually cushioned my fall. Nothing broke and I didn't split my lip because my chest made sure there was a crucial couple of inches distance between my face and the ground. I'm never going to be defensive about my size again. I posted my achievement online and almost immediately the responses poured in from chubbies whose fat had saved them from definite fractures.

You are an unfinished masterpiece and you hold the brush and palette in your hands. Life coaches tell you, you are unique. What's new about that? Do you know anyone else who looks like you, walks and talks like you, has the same strengths and flaws as you?

You are one of a kind. Good and bad, strengths and weaknesses are all part of this package that makes you who you are. (I can feel preachiness coming on and I do apologise, but I am writing this for you.) What I'm saying is only this. Live your life according to the essence that is you.

Do not allow random opinions to determine your path.

You know what your essence is? It is the person you were when you were two, three, four, five and six years old. You knew what you liked and what you did not like and you were not afraid to say it. You were not afraid to ask questions either and you asked them clearly and loudly.

Don't allow people to make you feel bad about yourself

The trouble begins when you allow people to get under your skin. Make no mistake about it, these are horrible people. They tell you that you are flawed and you beat yourself up over it. They say that they are trying to improve you, but they are just being petty and nasty. Do not allow them to do that.

Don't allow anyone else to intrude into your space, even if you agree with what they are saying. You are the only one who is qualified to work on yourself, or not, if you feel there's no need to. Warts and all, just be proud of who you are.

Look at Freddie Mercury, the front man of the iconic rock band *Queen*. He had a massive overbite, was teased about it and called names as he grew up, but he had a three, almost four, octave range to his voice and he was sure his overbite helped him somehow with that distinctive voice of his. He used his 'flaw' to rock the entire music-loving world.

Look at Peter Dinklage, an actor born with dwarfism, yet he is a giant in his field who commanded every scene he appeared in, in the series *Game of Thrones*. Look up his interviews on the internet. The struggles he went through in his life and how he dealt with problems is a beacon for all of us.

It makes no sense for you to brood over some aspect of your face or body, or character, or try desperately to hide it. It's there, accept it. Better still, embrace it because that is what sets you apart from the herd. That gives you, as far as I am concerned, a personality.

There was this editor of a magazine I once worked for. She was beautiful to look at, svelte, charming, gorgeous hair, expressive eyes, a beautiful smile with the deepest dimples, but her nose! I thought her nose was all wrong. It was large and slightly bent. I thought what a pity, she should totally get that nose fixed and she will look like a film star. But that nose was what gave her face character. If she went in for cosmetic surgery, she would have looked like a million other pretty women. When she walked into a room, heads turned.

She owned her space and everyone in the room acknowledged and respected that.

Perfection has nothing to do with happiness

My school teachers would point to high achievers in various fields and tell us to emulate them. I learned that that is a sucker's game. Read their biographies. Most high achievers have a very dark side, and in all probability, it is that dark side that helped them achieve that high status, but rarely popularity with their colleagues or family or friends.

All the perfectionists I know are miserable sods, expecting validation every step of the way. All of them. *Miserable*. What's worse is they cannot handle imperfections in those around them. The truly successful are generally ordinary individuals who had a talent, worked on it and swept the world off its feet.

Take out the clutter

The moment you are embarrassed about something and try to cover it up, you begin thinking you are not good enough. You begin thinking everyone else is better than you. You fade into the woodwork, or you pretend to be someone you are not. There is no need to punish yourself. Just take out the clutter.

Understand who you are, accept your strengths and your weaknesses with grace. Figure out your path in life and follow it. If you find a fascinating detour anywhere, follow it, but let it be your choice, not anyone else's.

If you spend your time surrounded by people who make

you feel small and useless, move away from them. Say 'no' to that which you dislike and refuse to go along with it. That's a giant step towards being in control of your personal space.

The key is to enjoy who you are

All that you need to do is be the best possible version of yourself and you'll find that you don't merely love yourself; you enjoy yourself. That's when you find happiness within you. That inner happiness attracts people, and when and if you zero in on someone who fits into your life, your relationship blooms and everything is tinged with joy.

When love comes calling, don't pretend to be someone you are not

It's a horror story when you are still not sure of whom you are and you fall in love. You think yes, this is The One and you pretend to be someone you are not. It is incredibly hard work living a lie for an indefinite period of time. If it is desperate love powering this lie, it is almost certainly going to end badly for you. So listen to me and get your own life sorted *before* looking around for The One.

He may be The One, or she may be The One, but you my friend, you are Number One. You have to be your own top priority. Many wet blankets will say that is selfish. But when it comes to your own life and your future, you have to be a taker. Be a giver when it is required, but when it is your own life and your own future, please be a taker.

Taking the rough with the smooth—Are you a taker or a giver?

If you take a look around, no two persons are ever equally committed to each other. There is always one who works harder at keeping the relationship working. That person will juggle their appointments to do something for the comfort and joy of the other.

The other is not that invested in the relationship. The invested partner is the giver, the uninvested is the taker. The giver does the heavy-lifting in the relationship, working hard to keep the taker happy.

The key lies in recognising your degree of dependence on your partner. If you are crazy about him and he is not that crazy about you, you're in for a great deal of frustration. You know he is not that crazy about you when every action of his points out to you being a low priority in his world.

He forgets to call you, or text. He gives you lame excuses or worse, no excuses at all. He spends more time at work or with his friends than with you. He doesn't know what you like and he doesn't really care that he doesn't know. He leaves you feeling off-balance and frustrated.

There you are prioritising him, laying down all the love and commitment you have in you, and all he does is scatter a few crumbs of affection your way. He is the light of your life, burning brightly, and you fly around him like a moth, burning your wings. Step away—he is not worth the effort.

The taker is just along for the ride. Being a giver is frustrating and, well, sad. When it comes to decisions affecting your own life, don't be the moth, be the flame. You need someone who prioritises you most of the time. I say 'most of the time' because you need to give each other space to grow comfortably together. The point is, he should not be making decisions for you without consulting you and you shouldn't be building your life around his priorities unless those are your priorities too.

If you know you are a magic carpet why be a doormat?

When we are overwhelmed by feelings of not being good enough, we turn ourselves into doormats and allow others to wipe their feet on us. That's fine if you are a natural-born doormat and it gives you fulfilment to have people walk all over you.

Perfectly wonderful people are doormats—caregivers, many mothers, many fathers. Sometimes doormats turn into serial murderers. They take being bullied as their normal and fit their life decisions around the bullying, even if that decision is serial murder. But most of us are not doormats.

Most of us are magical carpets, woven with fascinating colours from the finest yarn. We want to fly because we are built to fly. The trouble starts when a magical flying carpet pretends to be a doormat, and what good can come of that? It's a nuisance and a complete waste of time. Be yourself, do your thing, even if you haven't got a clue.

There is no point in trying to conform. All of us enjoy taking the occasional selfie—we all have a touch of the narcissist in us, wanting to look better than we actually do. But continuously hunting for validation is the chronic selfie-poster on social media. These are the textbook Givers.

Chronic selfie-clickers try so hard to conform to the norm, to be accepted, to be loved and admired. They are overly conscious of the correct angle to hold their heads when they smile for a selfie. Even the smile is practised. After the fourth try, they still look doubtful about whether any of the selfies should make it to their social media pages or be deleted.

Chronic selfie-takers, both men and women, are not textbook narcissists. I would say (and you may disagree with me—see if I care) that they are givers, with more than their fair share of insecurities, because they work so hard to conform to what they believe are the requirements of social media.

They are convinced that they must keep their friends and followers in the loop about the minutiae of their lives. What they eat, what they drink, what they wear, what they randomly feel at any time of day. They are convinced that people will read and marvel or sympathise and it hurts them deeply if no one acknowledges their post. In my view, these are not takers because they need constant validation.

Then there are those who don't try at all. They don't give a damn whether they conform or not. They dance to their own tune. They take being accepted as a given, because they accept themselves. They take life on their own terms. They are focused on what they need and set out to get it. These are the takers.

Sometimes I think about life and I compare it to a deranged monkey. Life has this unfortunate habit of flinging all sorts of stuff at us without prior warning—good things and unbelievable faecal matter. The choices we make will turn us into givers or takers.

To be exclusively a giver or a taker is not great because both extremes of character are truly annoying. In an ideal world, yes, there should be a balance of giving and taking, but studying our far from ideal world, I've stripped it down to this: when it comes to decisions that will directly affect your life and your future, you must be a taker and in control of your own space. When you are content with your choices, you have found your bliss.

Inner happiness and the art of getting along with others

When you find contentment in who you are, flaws and all, inner happiness becomes the signature of your soul. There is a kind of magic to that. It underlines every action you take. If you are your own best friend, there's little in the way of relationships that can mess with that. Inner happiness manifests in a cool self-assurance that attracts the right people. You don't have rigid plans for your future. You don't go hunting for love. Or wealth.

If we can get love and wealth too, we've got it made. What they don't tell us is that to get either of these, we have to sacrifice time, energy and peace of mind. At the end of the day, we miss those three things like you wouldn't believe.

If we are lucky, we might get one or the other—love or wealth. Maybe even both, but how many people nail both? I don't see many individuals happy with the choices they made. There are a few, very few, who are genuinely content but these are people who aspired to neither love nor wealth.

They weren't great-looking or especially brilliant. They just lucked in on love and wealth. They got along well with the people in their lives, they used the skills they had and worked at what they enjoyed. Their relationships too are fun and fulfilling.

That is one element you will always find in successful relationships: the couple gets along well. They get along with each other, with their children and their parents. Neither is too demanding or judgmental of the other, or of their children, or friends or neighbours, or colleagues.

Any idiot (and lord, their numbers keep increasing) can be negative and judgemental. Any idiot with a low IQ and a lower EQ can pull you down with ease, denigrate whatever you do, belittle every achievement of yours.

It takes a high level of intelligence, hard work and generosity of spirit to get along with people. Getting along, accepting family and friends, *their* warts and all, is really hard work but it makes for healthy and happy long-term relationships.

If all of us could just get along with each other, there would be no need for passports, terrorism or divorce lawyers. But we have thick egos and thin skins and we hold on to grudges like someone's going to steal them from us.

I say go with the flow. If you have been deliberately hurt by words, deeds, or physically through NO fault of your own, take no prisoners, never forgive and never forget. One presumes here that you are a normal person with normal insecurities, not a card-carrying psychopath.

Forgiving and forgetting makes no sense to me. Why run the risk of getting hurt all over again by the very same people? Not forgiving or forgetting does not mean you must hold grudges.

Holding a grudge is not smart. It involves negativity building up deep inside of you and that leads to all sorts of health issues.

Better to get mad, get even and then banish the person from your inner circle.

Clear the clutter from your mind and you will know what your endgame is and what needs to be done to get there. When you take a good look at your strengths and weaknesses, you can figure out what kind of partner will be good for you and what kind of people you want sharing your space.

Set up support systems by building strong friendships with people of different ages and interests. No matter what the pressure is on you to marry and settle down, or move in with a partner, first figure out what works for you in terms of contentment. Then you never have to chase after happiness. It springs from deep inside you and surrounds you like an energy field. Love who you are, before loving someone else. Then tell them who you are.

3

Use Dating for Eliminating

How does one know if he's lying about himself? Is this the Special One? Is he real or fake? Should this be casual or serious? I don't have the time to hunt for a date; should I try an online dating app or website?

One of the first things my first date said to me was astonishing. We ordered coffee and snacks and, suddenly, right out of the blue during our date, he looked a little to the left of my left eye, so he was probably speaking to my left ear, and he said this: 'What do you cows see in me.' It was not a question. It was a statement and I, who am rarely at a loss for words, was, to put it bluntly, at a loss for words.

I looked at him with some concern, and he smiled a beautiful smile and twinkled his beautiful eyes. Ordinarily, I would not have allowed a statement like that to go unchallenged. Essentially he was calling me a cow and clubbing me with all the alleged cows that gave him the glad eye. I should have gulped my cold coffee and flung *his* drink in his face, but like a complete airhead, I put that cow remark to pasture.

I convinced myself that I had heard wrong. But that date led to another and another and the cow motif appeared sporadically. I began objecting, and he stopped referring to girls as cows, but it was not the word that was the problem. That cow remark came out of a deep-rooted contempt for his female peers. Decades later he still shows the deepest contempt for women. And till today, whenever he wishes to be nasty, he speaks to my left ear. Yeah...I married him. Don't judge me, I was desperately in love.

A date is actually a sneak preview

Dust off that mental Bullshit Radar and keep it at your table when you go out on a date. You will see the gentleman on his best behaviour and you will also see behaviour he tries to hide. The signs are all there, you just have to look for them.

At some point or the other, we all feel an urgent need to find our significant other. The pressure builds up seeing a bunch of peers in serious relationships. Your family drops heavy settling-down hints, society and mass media tells you no one should be alone.

You find yourself considering a friend of a friend, or you think maybe the person you meet regularly during the day or week looks interesting, or you decide to sign up for a dating app and hope for the best.

You feel that quickening of the pulse when you see the

Special One. Your eyes meet. You feel a heightened awareness. Your brain is flashing you a constant signal: HE-is-the-one. HE-is-the-one. HE-is-the-one. Your heart is pumping that message through your body. There's chemistry between you. That's good. Now the work begins.

Begin with yourself. You know what you like and you know what turns you off. You will see how he conducts himself in public, with his friends and family, and on social media. You will also see his behaviour with your friends and family and finally, his behaviour when you two are alone with each other. You don't have to be in full Sherlock Holmes mode. Just be aware. Your first warning should be the moment you feel uncomfortable about something he says or does.

Your second and final warning is when you find yourself making excuses for him. That is the time to remove him from your personal space.

We date for one of two reasons: We want a fun couple of hours in the company of an entertaining person, or we go out with him because we think this could be The One.

Whatever your reason for seeing the guy, consult mutual friends before a first date. It's always nice to know that the guy is not a psychopath who could turn you into a police statistic the next day.

This is the best time of your life. You look your best. You feel your best. The whole world is at your feet. Romance is the perfect relaxation after a hairy day at work. And it is not just when you are young; romance rocks at any time of life.

You may be struggling to make a difference, or to move up the corporate ladder, or to just get that bump in your salary after appraisals. You need the break of a romantic dinner or a long drive, or just meeting for a coffee and having a few laughs. It brings balance into your life. You don't have to marry the guy, but if you do think he is The One, then below are a few pointers to help you eliminate the unworthy.

First, should you date many people at the same time or just one? The consensus is to date as many as you can. No need to jump into bed with any or all of them, keep it light and casual. Learn all you can about them and then do your eliminations without any drama.

The first date may work out well or it may be awkward. The second date is the important one; if it goes well, the third is taken for granted and you are on the high road to a relationship. If it does not work, you could have made a good friend for life and there's no such thing as having too many friends.

It's great to have friends who think like you do and a few who don't, to keep your mind elastic. They come in handy when you are in danger of making a complete jackass of yourself, like when you are desperately in love with someone who is completely wrong for you. Or you are desperate for a career you have no aptitude for.

While my dating knowledge is practically zero, since I married the cow guy, here's advice from friends who know what's what about dating.

They say you can read character during a date by taking note of body language, behaviour, intelligence, empathy, eating habits and financial street smarts. The tips they provide are not for a casual evening out, but for going out with the Special One you think you could go the distance with.

The first thing they spoke about is the scariest phenomenon today—online dating. So first, let's get online dating out of the way. These are their inputs. Preachy alert, but hey, the message. Focus on that.

Don't be too hasty in sharing personal contact details online

Rule number one, since there are too many swindlers and rapists out there, keep your personal contact details to yourself. Don't give any information that can lead people to your place of work or to your home. If they ask you, lie.

Any interaction should be restricted to chatting on the app itself. Yes, you do get genuine people looking for a genuine date but online sites are stamping grounds for stalkers, rapists and thieves.

These are highly skilled criminals, so why make their job easier for them? If the app makes it mandatory that you provide your location and anything that would allow a stranger to access you in your home, do not sign in to that app.

Search the internet for information about your date. Check if their photographs point to their real identity. Check their profiles and see what they like and what they share.

Do not invite your online date to collect you from your home. Take a taxi to and from the venue, or better still, ask a friend to drop you and collect you. Agree to meet at a crowded place and not an isolated romantic spot.

It's not merely rapists and psychopaths you have to worry about. Enough men and women have been conned into parting with most of their savings to crooks on dating sites and on regular social media too.

When people offer you rich financial rewards, or come at you with a hard luck story, here's a simple enough rule. As soon as money has to leave your hands, stop and just don't do it.

Now make a list of your priorities.

What would you never give up for him?

Your career? Your family? Your freedom as a single person? Your friends? Your pets? Your music, art or hobbies? Your religion? The foods you love? This is important so that you know what is important to you.

What would be a deal-breaker for you?

Someone who has no ambition or too much ambition? Someone who cannot make up his mind? Someone who refuses to commit to you exclusively? Someone who has no respect for women? Someone who wants to settle down immediately and get serious? Someone who disrespects you? A control freak?

Courtesy

If good manners are a priority with you, see how genuine he is. Good manners should be easy and unforced. You get three types of guys.

Those who open doors for you and step aside to let you pass before them in an automatic action of natural courtesy.

The second type exaggerates his actions and will have a snarky see-how-well-mannered-I-am-you-lucky-girl look on his face. Know that he is putting on a show for the date. He will dispense with the courtesy as soon as he's sure of you.

Then there is the third guy who is not used to opening doors for girls and pulling out chairs, or rising when you rise to go to the washroom. If he is doing all this with dogged determination, then know that he is earnestly trying to make a good impression on you and you could show appreciation, instead of taking it as your right.

The meal

Does he consult you on what and where you would like to eat? Are you particular about what you like to eat? Does he discuss the menu with you and take the trouble to order a great meal?

Speaking for myself, since the menu gods cursed me, I always ask the other person to select a meal for me. Even if a celebrated chef is running the place, the day I turn up and choose a meal will be the day his wife runs away with his best friend and the meal will suck. But this is not about me. This is about you.

How does your date behave with the waiter? Is he courteous to the guy or does he click his fingers and order the waiter, instead of ordering the food? Six months into your relationship, he could be treating you like that.

Are you comfortable with the way he eats? They say the way a man eats (also the way he drinks and dances) is the way he makes love, so how he eats could be important. Does he enjoy his meal, savouring the taste of every mouthful? Does he pick at his food, or gulp it down like a zoo animal at feeding time?

Date conversation

Is his conversation easy and interesting? He should be drawing you in to learn more about you and talk about himself too. Is he secretive? If he is deflecting questions about his personal life, then he's got something to hide. Or he is a very private person.

If, on the third date, getting information out of him is still like pulling teeth, revisit the idea of a serious relationship. Living with a secretive person is like walking on eggs. It doesn't end well.

Paying and tipping

If he checks the bill carefully, that's good. If he does not check the bill and just pays up, he is not careful about his money or he is embarrassed you may think he's stingy. So watch his bill checking for a couple of dates; if he blindly pays the bill at all times, then that's not good for the long haul.

His tipping will also point out to his financial smarts. If he is a lavish tipper, paying more than 20 percent of the bill, he is either trying to impress you or just poor in math.

After-dinner observations

Does he want to go for a slow stroll after the meal, if you have agreed to only the meal as a first date? A stroll is good (unless he frog-marches you down a dark alley). He likes your company and wants you to like him.

When he drops you back home, does he grab you like it is his right since he fed you a good meal? The quality of the kiss doesn't really matter. What matters is if you are comfortable with it, with touching him and being touched by him.

If you are edgy and trying hard to please him, if you feel revulsion, I don't have to tell you it's not going to work.

The 400 percent annoyance rule

You will be looking for things that you like about the guy, to convince yourself that you made the right choice. But do yourself a favour and also pay attention to things he says and does that bother you.

If anything about your date annoys or embarrasses you, imagine that annoyance increased 400 percent (ahem, if, say, he refers to women as cows) and see if you can live with that 400 percent for the rest of your life without going berserk.

You may be fascinated by someone who eats every meal like he has been starving for a week, or you may feel embarrassed by it. Maybe he keeps shaking his legs or maybe he is so tall and thin, he does that thing where he crosses his knees and winds one leg around the other and his foot tucks in around his ankle. Yeah, I hate that. Maybe his eyes never settle down long enough to make proper contact with yours. Maybe he sprays when he speaks. Maybe he prays when he speaks. Maybe he has a facial tic or some more regrettable mannerisms. Apply the 400 percent rule. Even if you think you are being petty.

Canvas your family's opinion

If you have been dating him for a month or so and you like what you see, take him home to meet your family. If he makes excuses to avoid meeting them, he is not that into you. If he agrees to meet them, pay attention to how he gets along with every member of your family. If pets are important to you, see if he is comfortable with your pets.

It is always clever to canvas your family's opinion. You will be looking out for his strengths. They will be looking out for everything that is wrong with him. If there is something they don't like, get mad, of course, but be smart and check up on it.

Are you comfortable with his friends and family?

When you marry, you don't just marry your spouse, you marry his family and friends too. So if they give you the creeps, walk away.

You need to know if your partner is controlled financially or emotionally by relatives, friends, mentors, or parents. If he is, walk away. Marriage comes with its own problems; if the two of you are going to be dependent on third and fourth parties after you marry, life is going to be very stressful, unless you are a moocher too.

Is he respectful of the women in his life?

Is he respectful of his female relatives, colleagues, friends and vendors? If he treats them with courtesy and respect, you are on to a good thing. If he is demanding of them and expects them to wait on him hand and foot, unless you love waiting on someone, hand and foot, dump him.

Pay attention to his opinion of women. If his conversation and behaviour point to a low opinion of women, revisit the idea of a relationship with him.

If you are a stickler for elegant interiors

Have a look at his residence if you have definite plans for your future home. That decor is something he will want to introduce into your house too. Take a look at his parents' house. That décor is something he is familiar with and will probably want in his future home. His bedroom will tell you a lot about him.

If he is a slob and you are not, it would mean you will have to pick up after him all your life. If you like art and he likes neon signs, there's going to be many hiccups there too. If you like disarray and he likes elegance, think twice. It's not the end of the world, but if decor is important to you, or to him, it can be pretty frustrating.

Do you find yourself making excuses for him?

Observe yourself. If you find you are making excuses for him, or you are avoiding conversation about behaviour you dislike, either address those issues, or end the relationship. This is especially difficult if your biological clock's desperate quest to nest is driving you on the hunt for a partner. Don't settle for any partner who does not fit the bill.

You and he as a unit

What qualities would you appreciate most in your partner? Does loving and caring resonate with you, or does it make you impatient? Does creative talent of high calibre move you? What would you look forward to doing with your partner most of all? Family time? Partying? Attending public events? Adventure and travelling the world? Enjoying the little things, like a roadside meal or a wonderful sunset together? What kind of movies do you enjoy together?

When sharing a serious problem, would you like a supportive hug and words of sympathy? Impossible out-of-the-box ideas that make you laugh? Would you like him to make you forget your problems by distracting you, playing music for you, or giving you a massage, or taking you out for a treat? Would you like him to discuss your problem and find a solution that will actually work?

Magnetism is for magnets...

This thing about opposites attracting works for magnets, not humans. People with similar tastes in food, entertainment, political affiliation, sports, movies and so on tend to get along much better than those who have little in common with each other. I cannot flog this often enough. 'Getting along' is the key to a long and loving relationship.

Does he blame others most of the time?

If he invariably blames others for his failures, dump him, because he will be no good at handling emergencies. When things go wrong, he will first look to lay the blame for the incident on someone before he takes any action. That 'someone' will almost always be you.

You want a partner who will swing into action alongside you to fix things, and who, once the crisis is solved, will go after the one who caused the emergency.

How does he spend?

If he lavishly spends all he has on you, you will both be miserable when the money runs out. If he is stingy and tries to cut corners and economises all the time, he will be unbearable six months into the marriage.

You need someone who can spend and who can also save. The same applies to you. If you are one of the world's big spenders, keep away from someone who prefers to save his resources.

Does he treat you differently in private and in public?

Is he respectful of your point of view, or condescending? Does he sulk when he does not get his way? Does he stop talking to you after a disagreement and freeze you out until you apologise? Does he look embarrassed to be out in public with you? Does he rush you past people he knows without introducing you to them? If he is, and you don't like it, do yourself a favour and let him go.

Is he violent, or does he threaten violence?

If he gets into a rage and hits you, lodge a police complaint and leave. Do not make the mistake of thinking the assault was a one-off thing. No matter if you aggravated him and he begged your forgiveness and swore he would never do it again. Even if he weeps. Don't stay.

Never make excuses for a man who hits you. If he hits you once, he will hit you again, and again. No relationship is worth that kind of pain and humiliation.

What downloads and shares does he have on his social media accounts?

The Internet has made some things really easy to figure out. You can for instance get a pretty clear picture of what your potential partner likes and dislikes by just checking their social media pages. Even better if you can have a look at the downloads on his phone.

I can hear you say, have you gone mad, old woman, this is invasion of his privacy. Meh, is what I say. All's fair in love and war. Use the element of surprise and ask him to show you the videos and files he saves. Offer to give him your phone too, unless you have dark and dirty secrets. If he refuses, take a step back. The point is, you can see whether the two of you have common ground, common likes, common interests. Unless he is a scholar or professional doing research for a project, downloads rarely lie. If whatever interests him disgusts or worries you, well you know what you should do.

How do you recognise that your partner is cheating on you?

- The first red alert would be the calls that are very casually but immediately cut, or he hurries out of the room to speak, saying that it is work.
- He works late at the office, or at meetings in hotels and other companies.
- He is too tired to have sex with you and his work is not that physically taxing.
- Anything that makes you pause and struggle to find excuses for his behaviour.
- The easiest is to follow the money trail, but if you have reached this stage in your relationship, then call it off. Marriage requires trust and open lines of communication.

Adam Lodolce, author of *Men Love Confident Women*, puts it in a nutshell. He says when you go on a date there are seven pointers you have to be aware of about yourself:

1. You are just not happy when you are with him.
2. He makes you feel bad about yourself.
3. Unbiased people are telling you to get out of the relationship.
4. You are constantly thinking about other guys and wishing he were like them.
5. You are constantly wishing you were still single.
6. You are always making excuses for his bad behaviour.
7. Your gut tells you he is not right for you. Trust your gut.

The rest is easy. If you like travel, adventure, food and music, look for someone who loves it too. If you prefer sitting at home doing cosy home things, don't hook up with someone who loves the great outdoors or wants to check out the newest restaurant in town or catch the first day first show of any film or play hitting town. Marriage or a long-term live-in relationship is fun when you share the same interests. It's easier to get along too. Trust me, I know what I'm talking about because I'm old, I'm wise and I *know* my shit.

4

Sex Is Great but Your First Time Is a Mess

Your parents tell you you'd better not get pregnant and ruin your life. Your boyfriend wants to 'take it to the next level' and have sex. Your peers have all had sex and they are not pregnant or HIV positive. You are tired of being laughed at for being a virgin.

If people tell you sex is great, well, yes, it is, only if you are with someone who knows what he is doing and if you know what you are doing. But if it is your first time, everyone, unless they are big fat liars, will tell you that the first time is horrible, embarrassing and cringeworthy. My first sexual experience, like most people's, was clumsy, painful and very embarrassing. Perseverance, a sense of the comical in trying to figure out this basic activity of all living things, however, paid off and sex became something quite brilliant.

Sex is a fact of life because all living things are sexual beings, more so, teenage girls and boys. My first instinct is to tell all teens to never have sex at all. I wish I could tell them that they will get pregnant and get an STD right off the bat, but I won't say that because sex is wonderful. It is not dirty. It is not disgusting. How can it be disgusting when it is the source of creation and it does wonderful things for your neurotransmitters and your mental equilibrium?

Having said that (preachy alert, but hey, the message...), being sexually active in your teens is not such a great idea. Not because of pregnancy and STDs—good quality condoms sort that out—but because your mind and your body are not quite ready for the magnitude of such an activity.

Still, no matter how much adults and society tell you not to have sex, you are going to want to do it. You hear plenty about how not to get pregnant, how not to get STDs, and society tells you to say no to sex before you are married, or eighteen.

Today's sexual activity, even if it is a one-off thing, carries all the old risks and a major new one. You could find your sexual experience becoming an internet sensation. Maybe you can take videos of you and your sexual partner going viral in your stride. Maybe you don't mind if your relatives and friends, potential employers and colleagues have something to laugh and gossip about, but a number of suicides have happened as a result of this unfortunate video-shooting habit of some pieces of slime.

You could go along with that and stay virgin till you marry, but one day you will decide to have sex before or after marriage and you will need to equip yourself with correct information. Yeah, I'm preaching, but this is important. Like most teens, you will get your information from porn.

You may have watched porn, or your partner may have watched porn and is expecting action along those lines from you. Remember, porn is fiction, like wrestling shows. Those are professionals playing roles. Those are not real sexual relationships. That 'Oh god, oh god, oh god, I'm coming' business is scripted, and quite funny really. A real orgasm or multiple orgasms is one of the most fabulous feelings in the world. From your toes to your scalp, your entire body experiences that orgasm. In the real world, enjoyable sex doesn't just magically happen. Practice with your partner makes perfect.

Your first experience will be fumbling, awkward, painful even. It helps to talk with your partner about sex. Don't stress over it, laugh together about it and figure out what needs to be done. It should be fun and pleasurable for both of you. This takes exploration and doing what you feel comfortable doing. When you both talk, there should be complete honesty between your partner and you.

Your partner may want to do things you are not comfortable with. When that happens, your job is to say 'No' without feeling guilty about it. If something doesn't feel right, speak out.

It's not the end of the world if you find sex uncomfortable; there are lubricants, cold creams, petroleum jelly, and various pure oils to prevent bruising in and around your vagina. If you feel any injury or pain, tell him clearly. If he is unconcerned about your discomfort, dump him. You need to know what you like and what you don't, before you learn what he likes and what he does not.

Masturbation helps you discover the erogenous zones of your body

This brings us to the issue very few people talk about—masturbation. This is normal and necessary for girls as well as boys. I'm not the only one saying this. Jane Epstein, a nurse practitioner who works at the University of New Mexico and specialises in adolescent medicine, delivered a TEDx talk where she says it is time to talk to teenage girls about sex. Jane Epstein provides contraceptive and sexual health-care services to teenagers. Her focus is to help young women feel empowered about their health, their choices and their sexuality.

Masturbation, she says, helps you learn about your body and you learn what brings you to orgasm. It's important for you to know your own body, to know how to enjoy sex with yourself before having sex with another person.

Masturbation gives you first-hand information about pleasuring your body, which you should pass on to your partner. Your partner, no matter how practiced he is in the art of sex, will still be groping in the dark when it comes to pleasuring you. Once you know your erogenous zones, tell him where they are; and he will share his preferences with you. Masturbation allows you both to better understand your wants and needs.

There are five or six major erogenous zones and an unlimited number of secondary erogenous zones in a woman's body. Every individual has some out of the ordinary erogenous zones, so it's basically wherever you feel ticklish.

It could be your ears or earlobes, your eyelids, your forehead, your lips, your underarms, below your breasts, the inside of your upper arms, your wrists, your fingertips, your abdomen, your navel, the small of your back, your butt cheeks, the inner thigh, the arch of the foot and the toes.

The major erogenous zones are the ones most involved in intercourse—nipples, clitoris, G-spot, cervix, the opening of the vagina and the anus.

Experimenting with different erogenous zones by touching them with the lightest of touches will teach you what gives you maximum pleasure. Find your partner's erogenous zones and share information. Sex, like all other aspects of a relationship, improves with proper communication. That makes for a level of honesty in your relationship that can only enrich your life together.

You owe it to yourself to get up-to-date factual information on sex

Sex is healthy and empowers an individual but it is an adult activity, and you need to go into it fully aware of what you are doing. The fallout can throw your life completely out of gear.

If you are thinking of having sex when you are in your teens, you know your parents would find the idea gross, but you owe it to yourself to get up-to-date information on birth control. If you cannot talk to your parents or any adult relative, talk to your doctor about birth control. If you cannot talk to a doctor, your path to safe sex is simple: just insist that your partner slip a condom over his penis before he slips his penis into you.

Learn to say a definite 'no' and a definite 'yes'

Before the decision to engage in sexual activity, you need to sharpen your decision-making skills. First factor in what's good for your body and what's good for your life. Let there be no negotiation on that. Set healthy boundaries around yourself and let your peers know those boundaries.

Girl, once you develop assertiveness in yourself, that's power there. Assertiveness that you will go this far and no further is a skill you must develop. You can avoid a whole bunch of messy life situations if you know how to say a definite 'no' and a definite 'yes'.

It's even better if you have a partner who can accept a definite no and a definite yes. Assertiveness comes hand in hand with negotiating skills, which help you to give and receive consent without dithering. In this way you develop a healthy, open and trustful relationship with your partner.

You deserve to have sex that thrills you. You deserve to have sex that is not harmful and that is not abusive. You deserve to have sex that you can ask for without being afraid of rejection. You deserve to be in a sexual relationship where you can have clear discussions on going together to a clinic and getting tested. Sex is not a game; it is a responsibility. It can be dangerous to your health and it can put the brakes on any dreams you have for your life ahead. So, sharpen those decision-making skills. Know where you want to go and what works for you.

Health benefits of sex

Sex with a partner we love has amazing health benefits. They say those who enjoy sex with their partner live longer and healthier lives, but maybe it is the bonding and love that causes longevity. I am not too sure that it could be sex alone. Nuns in a convent live to a ripe old age, but experts say a good sexual relationship is good for health, so let's take their word for it with slight reservation. They say people in sexual relationships have increased desirability, self-confidence, better relationships and greater happiness.

According to sex therapist Dr Zhana Vrangalova, who has a PhD in developmental psychology from Cornell University, sex sets off a cascade of neurochemical processes in the brain that lead to love. Some neurotransmitters released during sex are oxytocin, vasopressin and dopamine, which help two partners to bond with each other. The more you have sex with that person, the stronger that bond grows. So okay, sex keeps you young when you're old and it keeps you happy.

The first time is generally awful and truly underwhelming

Let's first dispel the myth that is 'virginity'. It's not a biological concept. It's a social one, created and perpetuated over the centuries for the sole purpose of keeping women under control. Imposing imagined ideas of 'purity' on women's bodies is an age-old trick. Occasionally, I wonder about the comic who named the tissue that society has been claiming for centuries, morphs a girl into a woman. They must have had a weird sense of humour. Hymen. Was that a cheery greeting to men?

A hymen, for those at the back, is a perfectly useless ring of small tissue that is such a major social issue. Did you know that not all women are born with a hymen? And if you do have a hymen, it's not a 'wall' at the mouth of your vagina to be bulldozed by a penis.

It is not a membrane and it does not cover the opening of the vagina. If it does, it's an exception to the rule and what's more, it will block your menstrual flow. This means you will have to go to a gynaecologist and get it opened to let the menstrual blood out.

A hymen is just a stretchy tissue and therefore does not 'break' during penetrative sex. It simply stretches, like a scrunchy. And because it's a tissue, a bruised hymen heals. This means that it is impossible to tell by simply looking or feeling a vagina if a woman has had sex or not. So the medieval idea that penetration somehow permanently changes things in a body with a vagina is something your Bullshit Radar should warn you against.

Laci Green the cheery young YouTube sex educator has been making informational videos about everything dealing with being sexually active. She has videos discussing body image, slut-shaming, genital hygiene and finding the G-spot. Her video on the hymen has been the most popular. She's cute and funny and tackles ticklish feminine and societal problems with ease. You will learn from her too that the hymen isn't a membrane that entirely covers the mouth of the vagina. It is just a small tissue of usually elastic folds that is located 1–2 cm inside the opening of the vagina. It stretches. It rarely tears. It is also referred to as the vaginal corona.

If you want even more easy-to-understand info on the vaginal corona aka hymen and virginity, as well as illustrations of some of the different ways hymens can look, check out **scarleteen.com**

I could tell you that the act of sex is when a penis enters a vagina, but that's giving too much credit to the little fellow. There are different kinds of sex, and you get to define what sex is to you—it just has to be safe, consensual and pleasurable.

One fine day you may decide to have sexual intercourse for the first time. Maybe you met someone with whom the chemistry is right, maybe you are curious, or maybe you just decide it's time.

Your first sexual experience could be of any type, oral, or digital (using fingers or toes), or anal, or mutual masturbation, or could involve the use of vibrators, dildos and sex toys. Your partner may be a person with a penis or a person with a vagina or an intersex person. What's important is that you give time to discover your and your partner's erogenous zones and enjoy as much foreplay as you like.

A majority of women do not bleed during their 'first time'. If you do bleed after intercourse, it's because you weren't sexually aroused or lubricated enough, so the friction caused minor bruises on the vaginal wall or, occasionally, the hymen tissue. This can happen any time you have penetrative sex by the way, not just during your first time.

If you and your partner are completely comfortable with each other and know how to stimulate each other, you may be able to orgasm, but most often, the first time is a lot of sloppy fumbling and thrusting, so don't get your hopes up.

Ask any woman about their first sexual experience and the

answer would be an average 1 or even a minus 9 on a pleasure meter of 1 to 10. Like with anything else, you get better at it as you practice with your partner.

Sexual activity is an adult activity that comes with adult problems. Condoms work most times, but sometimes they don't. The birth-control pill works most times; sometimes it doesn't. Pulling out before ejaculation works once in a blue moon; most times it doesn't.

If you are sexually active, carry a couple of condoms in your purse.

If your partner holds you in a close embrace and whispers huskily that you should not worry, they will pull out on time, tell them clearly, no, they must use a condom. If he doesn't have one, give him one. It is your body. You take control of it. What goes into it has to be your decision; not your partner's.

And that's the bare bones of your first sexual encounter. The rest—the date, the candlelit dinner, the wine, the roses, the picnic, the movie, the dancing, the kissing, the fondling, the intimacy, the bedroom, the morning after—those are all peripherals.

It's funny how, before you get your driving licence, you are taught to recognise signals, dangers of driving, rules of the road, penalties for breaking said rules and, best of all, you actually learn how to drive your vehicle. Yet for sexual activity, there is no school or licence available; you have to pick it up as you go along. Sex education in schools is generally festooned with morality lectures and clinical knowledge. They don't speak of the sexual act itself, or the pleasure it gives. They don't tell you of different types of sexuality, or different types of sexual experience. Yet, if anyone started a school for sex, they'd probably be arrested on the spot.

High-risk 'cool' sexual activity with multiple partners is adventurous, makes you popular, gives you self-confidence and so on, but it can be dangerous. There is enough information out there for you to be aware of the perils of irresponsible sex. Men are hit with paternity suits, but women are hit with pregnancy, labour and delivery, raising the child and struggling to survive. Not to mention the numerous sexually transmitted infections (STIs) one can be stuck with.

It is not worth the risk to be counted among the cool kids. It is definitely not worth the risk so that you can 'prove' your desperate love for some idiot. A condom has to be *de rigueur* if your partner wants to have sex with you. Now to be a really cool kid, you could look into the HPV vaccination, which helps prevent cervical cancer. The human papilloma virus is sexually transmitted, but both you and your partner can get vaccinated against it.

Sources:

https://www.theatlantic.com/health/archive/2014/02/living-myths-about-virginity/283628/

https://www.chicagotribune.com/redeye/ct-redeye-ask-anna-vaginal-hymen-myths-misconceptions-sex-20191028-tod3ngltlvht7gxhpuv7gn3pbu-story.html

https://www.scarleteen.com/article/bodies/my_corona_the_anatomy_formerly_known_as_the_hymen_the_myths_that_surround_it

Contraception is not always 100 percent effective

Contraception is effective when you use it correctly. When you use it wrongly, like missing a pill or getting the injection too late, then you could get pregnant. The UK NHS website https://www.nhs.uk/conditions/contraception/how-effective-contraception/ reviewed in April 2020, has a very clear set of comparisons of different types of contraception. You can see which one is available in your part of the world and how it is to be used.

Some methods are more effective than others. You need to follow the instructions and use your contraception correctly for it to be as effective as possible. There are some methods which are foolproof such as the implant. No contraception is 100 percent reliable. Some can have side effects.

- There are the long-acting reversible contraceptive (LARC) methods, where you cannot go wrong since these are surgically inserted into your body. The implant is more than 99% effective. It works for three years and can be taken out earlier.
- Intrauterine system (IUS): More than 99% effective. An IUS normally works for 3 to 5 years depending on the type, but can be taken out earlier.
- Intrauterine device (IUD): More than 99% effective. An IUD can stay in place for 5 or 10 years depending on the type, but can be taken out at any time.
- Contraceptive injection: It lasts for 8 to 13 weeks depending on the type. These have to be used regularly;

when they are not used regularly they are only 94% effective.

- Contraceptive patch: If used correctly it is more than 99% effective. If used wrongly it is only 91% effective, i.e., 9 women in 100 will get pregnant.
- Vaginal ring: This is 99% effective. If used wrongly it is 91% effective.
- Combined contraceptive pill is 99% effective but if you miss a pill the effectiveness is 91%.
- Progestogen-only pill is 99% effective but 91% effective if you don't take it regularly.
- Female sterilisation: More than 99% effective.
- Male sterilisation or vasectomy: Around 1 in 2,000 men can become fertile again in their lifetime after a vasectomy.
- Male condoms are 98% effective, if used wrongly male condoms are only 82% effective.
- Female condoms are 95% effective, if used wrongly they are around 79% effective.
- Diaphragms and caps are 92 to 96% effective. If used incorrectly effectiveness drops to 71 to 88%.
- Natural family planning, if followed precisely, is 99% effective. But following it precisely includes monitoring cervical secretions and basal body temperature. If used incorrectly it is 76% effective, which means 24 in 100 women will get pregnant in a year.

  [Source: NHS UK]

Go in for sex when you are good and ready, not earlier

Are you worried about peer pressure? That's easy to handle. Read up on sex and tell them that you had sex for the first time in your life when you went off on holiday and met this gorgeous guy. They're not going to check. There's no way they can check. Make sure you tell them it was no fun at all. Then they will believe you really did get hot and heavy with some guy.

Just be smart. Pay attention to protecting yourself. Protect your body from being used as a semen-disposal bin. Protect yourself from being brainwashed by peers and people wanting to get inside your pants. 'Deflowering' a virgin or 'popping her cherry' is supposed to be a good sport for some cretins. Have sex when you are good and ready; do not ever be forced or coaxed into it. You have to go into it with full awareness of the joy as well as the risk involved.

Sex seems to be different for boys

Maybe it is the indoctrination received by girls that sex outside and before marriage is a no-no, sluttish and shameful, while boys' overt sexuality is smiled upon as manliness in the proud tradition of the patriarchal society they live in. If they misuse their sexuality they are famously pardoned with the excuse: Boys will be boys.

The girl is constantly reminded that her 'value' as a member of society and potential wife and mother to one man, is to be good and not a 'slut' until she is given in marriage to that one man. She is not allowed to view sex as something pleasurable.

The boy is encouraged to have as many sexual encounters as he likes and he gets stud status.

Look at the positioning of the knees as accepted by society, girls are told to sit with their knees and feet together; boys are called effeminate if they sit like that, or even cross their knees. They are meant to sit or lounge with their knees apart and feet apart too.

This social indoctrination has affected natural sexuality in women around most parts of the world, since most parts of the world have patriarchal societies.

Girls should keep in mind that for most boys, sex is their top priority, nothing more, nothing less. For most girls, sex is a declaration of their commitment and love.

The girl's first sexual experience is a layered thing. With boys and men, initially it is the physical sexual act itself that is important. Society, in most cases, has wired them that way. Love and commitment may or may not come later. With the girl, it becomes a question of bonding with the boy she believes is the love of her life. She is giving and expecting serious commitment after that first sexual experience.

Having sex with the boy, allowing his penis to enter her vagina is to my mind, the equivalent of giving him a ring—who knows, maybe that is the symbolism of a wedding ring.

The virgin who was tired of being laughed at

This pretty young thing informed me that she was fed up of her parents protecting her, practically keeping her under house arrest. She said she was sick of her peers laughing at her and making loud comments about her virginity. She told me she wanted 'to just get laid' and be done with it.

'Being a virgin is a nuisance and I don't see what the big deal is,' she told me. She wasn't fearful or shrinking, just impatient to get it over and done with. I told her it was not a big deal, but I told her to first be aware of what protection she needed so she didn't get knocked up or catch a transmittable sexual disease, because *that* is a big deal.

She laughed in my face and told me everyone was doing it and they weren't knocked up or laid low with an STD. I said, 'Yeah, everyone is *telling* you that they are doing it. How do you know for sure? And if you have some guy in mind, how do you know he is clean?'

She laughed again, this time, 'You want me to take him to get a blood test to find out if he has an STD or AIDS?'

'Excellent idea,' I said. 'The results will take a month. Meanwhile read up on sex and birth control. Get all the information you need. It's only right and fitting that you get him tested. If you are going to shed blood for him, let him shed some for you. And for chrissakes make sure he wears a condom.'

I don't know if she took my advice. My job was to put the facts before her. After that it was her choice entirely.

5

The Four-Element Happiness Formula

Complete comfort with each other
Friendship
Respect
Trust

When I crossed the age of eighteen, remarkably dumb in matters of the world but quite abreast in rock music and classical English literature, I found to my great worry that I was as yet unattached. I had not fallen in love and no one had fallen in love with me.

To make matters worse, in our Literature class, we were reading that creepy poem *To His Coy Mistress* by Andrew Marvell addressed to some girl he had the hots for. The thrust of the poem was if she held onto her virginity for too long, she would die a virgin and the worms would get at her virginity and some such guff along the same lines. At eighteen it gave you pause.

That poem still pisses me off. If you ask me, it is the classic prelude to a #MeToo headliner. But never mind Marvell. The stories of my peers all around me were quite different, though.

All of them were falling in love like skittles—girls and boys, straight and gay—all acquired significant others. No danger of worms getting at lady or gentleman parts. Assorted relatives were getting married and I was getting invitations to their weddings.

Suddenly my pursuit of a career, professional training and a job was not so important anymore. Why the hell was I not falling in love with anyone? Was I destined to never find happiness?

See what happened? I began equating happiness with falling in love. I was already a happy person, but all the signals around me from peers and society were telling me otherwise and I believed those signals.

I felt short-changed. The radio and music systems played the greatest love songs mocking my aloneness. Even the advertisements were replete with loving couples and families. The discotheques were full of couples plastered to each other while I was head-banging to the gods of rock.

It was in this ridiculous mental condition that I met and fell in love with a boy who, I sincerely believed at the time, made the earth shake under my feet and the stars light up the sky. *Of course* I married the first person who caught my fancy. Never do that, sweetness. Wait. Watch. Observe how the relationship makes you feel.

More than success, more than wealth, more than health, all that any of us want, is to be happy. Some of us murder and steal and lie and cheat to find our happiness. Most of us just blunder through bewildered, hoping for the best.

I have learned that the trick lies in managing our expectations.

Have you ever seen newly hatched baby turtles rushing down the beach to the sea? It's scary how humans' pursuit of happiness is so like baby turtles blindly racing down to the ocean for food and survival. Humans have layered needs, so our pursuit of happiness is more complicated.

For us happiness is a package deal. It includes a whole lot of things for us. We want love, success, health, wealth, creature comforts, support systems, children, family, friends, community support, freedom and no pain. We are pulled in several directions in our dash towards our sea of happiness. Turtles just want survival.

As in the case of the turtle hatchlings, tragically, most of us humans end up with all sorts of predators and accidents that stop us from getting to where we are headed. But we are tougher than baby turtles; we don't get killed as easily. We continue to find ways and means to reach our bliss.

When we are kids, we are taught about truth and honour, courage and generosity but life throws curveballs at us where solutions are all about lies and dishonour, cowardice and selfishness. So we blunder through trying to find some middle path that can lead us through the mess with as much grace and as little pain as possible.

We go through all sorts of human relationships from kindergarten through high school, university, professional courses and skills training. We struggle to get that job and once we get it, it's a daily battle to hold on to it. Then we get laid off and we have to deal with depression and rage, finding another job or another career and the wheel keeps turning.

If we don't have a broad support system around us in terms of close friends and family, we're screwed. They provide vital stability and support. Looking at those saps you'd never think it, but close friends and family are vital for our mental health.

We hunt for love and passion but we put too much stress on the short term. We hook up with people who seem right but turn out all wrong. I can hear you saying, enough with the negatives, what makes for a lasting, committed, loving relationship?

I'll tell you, because I am old and wise. It is the bedrock of four non-negotiable elements: complete comfort with each other, friendship, respect and trust. If these are shared between two persons, it forms a forcefield around your relationship. Far from your relationship being on the rocks, it becomes the rock of your existence.

Statutory notice: This force field works only when all four elements are reciprocated by both partners.

What about passion, you ask? I'll tell you, because, well... you know... old...? Wise...? Passion is the fancy tooled-leather suitcase you carry your force field in. No matter how fancy, that suitcase is only an accessory. The nature of a suitcase is such that it is put away after you reach where you want to go. The forcefield you have inside the passion suitcase is what you need for happiness. Complete comfort with each other. Friendship. Respect. Trust. That's the lasting love combination.

Desperate besotted love is merely the suitcase. You pick it up when you want adventure and excitement. If the forcefield isn't packed into it, you're left feeling like a fool with a beautiful but empty suitcase. The desperate passion so many of us are determined to get at all costs, usually costs us and after it's over, you see how empty it is, like the suitcase.

The ancient science of Yoga speaks of three things to find your bliss in whatever you are doing at any given moment in time, whether it is work, or play or loving another:

- Do it to the best of your ability
- Do it without hurting others
- Do it without hurting yourself

Some researchers say Yoga is a ten-thousand-year-old science. It still works (we even have an International Yoga Day), so those yogis must have known what they were talking about when they tied themselves into knots way back when. These three pointers in life would apply to relationships equally. There's work in a relationship, so give it your best without hurting your significant other or yourself.

I have a question: When your partner enters a room, what do you feel? Do you feel proud, horny, possessive and joyful at the same time? Is it

(A) a boiling roiling combination?

Or

(B) a calm gentle melding of all those feelings?

The first one (A) is great fun, but no one can sustain that level of intensity. But (B)? That's the one that lasts.

With all the crap life chucks at us every step of the way, a support system of a partner, or husband, close friends and close family is something you have to work on. It does not happen automatically. Journalist and writer Sucheta Potnis, who read this over, has this to say: 'If you want support, you must be willing to ask for it. Once you acknowledge that you need support, and believe me, you will come across these situations many, *many* times, don't feel hesitant to ask for it. Even the strongest folks need support. So go ahead, don't feel shy. Ask for it and be happy to receive it. Support is a two-way street. There will come a time when your friends and family may also need support from *you*. When you ask, be prepared to offer it too.' Yeah, Sucheta is old and wise.

Once you build your support network of human relationships around you, you will find it easy to turn life's crap into rich fertilizer for personal growth.

How do you find the right person? First you focus on yourself. Understand who you are, what you need and what you can offer. Then look for someone who matches who you are. After that read the Compatibility Questionnaire in Part II, Chapter 6, and your answers will make three things abundantly clear: what you want, what you don't want and what you are prepared to offer your significant other.

Part II

Protection From Pain At Any Age

Content warning: Contains references to physical and mental abuse.

1

Warning Signs of an Unhealthy Relationship

Do you obsess about your partner every waking moment? Do all your decisions and actions revolve around making him happy because when he is happy you are ecstatic? Are you terrified of losing him?

When you see a dog in your path, you can tell if it is friendly or getting ready to sample the fleshy part of your calf. You see a snake, you know it won't attack you, unless you provoke it. With humans you cannot read a person's character in the first moments of meeting. Humans are a complicated bunch and peeling off the layers takes time and observation. Easier said than done, you will say. What do you look for, old woman? There are signs. There are always signs. You just have to look for them.

Early signals

Recognise the signs that quietly tell you the guy for whom your heart is doing mega bungee jumps may turn out to be a jerk of the highest order. The subtle indicators are there. Keep an eye out for any behaviour that leaves you frustrated, upset and resentful most of the time. This is your mind telling you that something is wrong. It means that one or more of your emotional needs are not being met.

Praying and hoping is one way to go, but if someone is consistently not giving you what you are looking for, then he is the wrong partner for you. He will not change. Most people may change temporarily but they will soon settle back into their true nature.

Here are some early signs to recognise that this relationship is not healthy for you. I've made a list of twenty warning signals you can keep an eye out for.

It starts with the little things. If they become a pattern, don't hope for the best for forty years. Dump him. If you cannot, then write him off as a roommate from hell and set about slowly but deliberately getting your own life on track. Now check for the following signs of a bad relationship:

1. You don't enjoy time together anymore and share nothing positive.
2. You feel lonely in your relationship and you feel awful when you compare other relationships with your own.
3. You are doing all the heavy-lifting in the relationship and he just can't be bothered. Yet the moment you stop doing things to make him happy, he makes you feel guilty.

4. You find there are several issues you just cannot talk about. You find yourselves fighting constantly, insulting, threatening or screaming.
5. You never text or talk to your friends in front of him. You also find yourself lying about meeting with friends or colleagues for a movie or a party because he will get mad.
6. He does not tell you where he is going, does not keep appointments with you and does not offer any explanation either.
7. You feel guilty when you spend time with your friends and family—that should be a clue that all is not well in your relationship. Alarm bells MUST ring when he tries to cut you away from your family and friends.
8. Something is wrong when your emotional state is entirely dependent on your partner. When he is happy, you are ecstatic; when he is angry, you are fearful and miserable.
9. He imposes his will on you, telling you that you must do things his way or get out of his life. You are supposed to be in a partnership, not in an owner–slave relationship.
10. He pisses all over your hopes and dreams and is condescending or tells you outright that your hopes and dreams are stupid.
11. He makes you feel bad about your body and holds others up as examples for you to follow. You end up feeling worse about yourself than when the relationship began.
12. He met you after a breakup and he obsesses about his ex. This means he is not emotionally invested in you.
13. He is constantly calling you or texting you to find out where you are and what you are doing.
14. You have almost broken up, or broken up more than once.

And your making up doesn't show that the see-sawing is ever going to stop. People don't change.

15. You turn to other people for emotional support but not to your partner because he cannot be bothered about things that are important to you.
16. He feels his problems are more important than yours.
17. You have differences in values regarding where you would like to live, city or country, whether you would like to have children, and in your views on finances.
18. If there are certain things you want to say to each other but can only say it in text messages and not face to face, that's a trust issue right there.
19. You worry about physical violence.
20. You feel hopeless about the future.

Do a fact-check on what you feel. Is it desperate love you feel? Do thoughts of him actively fill every moment of your day? Do you have manic swings of ecstasy and misery after he says or does anything? Do you feel drawn to him by some greater power you think is true love, but in actual fact is your need to experience what *you* believe is legendary love? Step back and think about what it is going to be like six months from now, or a year later. Know that it is only going to get worse and end the relationship quickly.

Desperate love only gets you fucked

Preachy alert, but hey, this is the voice of experience talking. Desperate love cannot be seen, measured, tasted or smelled, yet it holds us in thrall. Once we love anything or anyone to that point of desperation, objectivity flies right out the window and we sign away all claims to sanity.

Depending on the growing intensity of our love, the world shrinks at warp speed to a bubble around ourselves. We become blind to the world but the world has problems with our blindness and tells us so, especially family and friends whom we abandon once we find this great love of our life.

Many of us aspire to desperate love and in a classic case of 'be careful what you wish for' we generally get it. Whatever your sexual orientation and wherever you identify yourself on the gender spectrum, desperate besotted love follows a trajectory—there's ecstasy, extremes of highs and lows, agony, disillusion, mind games, emotional blackmail and resentment.

It is a blazing comet that fizzles out once the dreariness of household routine sets in. This does not happen with the non-desperate love that grows and deepens with every passing year and actually thrives on routine. Steady love begins as something warm and comfortable and keeps deepening.

But we want legendary love. We want the love that makes our eyeballs spring out of their sockets and our tongues roll out like a red carpet when we first see our love interest.

The best way to preserve the love in desperate love is to slowly remove the desperation. You can build on that love and turn it into a rock-steady relationship—one that will not throw you off-balance every time your partner frowns.

You can dispense with the desperation by stepping back and dialling it down a little. Keep some time aside so you can relax with friends and family, because being desperately in love saps your energy. Get back to giving time to other activities and people you love. Get your life back. Begin caring about how your actions affect you, *not* your lover. Begin caring for yourself because no one else is going to do it for you.

In any major agenda that comes up, position yourself in the centre of whatever action you plan to take, only then factor in your significant other. It is the only sensible thing to do. Look on it as mental-health insurance.

2

Zero Tolerance for Disrespect

Does your significant other talk down to you? Does he ridicule and humiliate you? Is he offensive to people dear to you? Do you keep silent when he behaves like a turd?

You know someone is disrespecting you when their words or actions make you feel bad about yourself. You can see they are aware of your hurt and distress but they go ahead and do it regardless. They are not teasing you. They are not pointing out your flaws to make you a better person. They are not offering you constructive criticism. They want to make you feel less than you are. These are bullies and you would do well to steer clear of them.

It gets hairy if this is how your significant other is treating you, but there are solutions. Manage your expectations. It's not too difficult and the benefits are huge. You accept the situation and do not look for someone to blame. Blaming someone even if it is their fault is a complete waste of time because it serves no purpose. A short-term vindication would be to mix some powerful laxative into his meal because if he is so full of crap, it's time he shed some of it, right? Joking, just joking.

You are uncertain and this uncertainty begins in your mind and the discerning eye sees it in your body language. You know who has a discerning eye? Every bully and control freak. They can sniff out self-doubt anywhere and they feed on it.

Bullied individuals try to cover up that uncertainty by becoming people-pleasers. If you are one such, it makes you a sitting duck for someone who has control issues. You find yourself doing and saying things you don't want to because you are afraid of offending people. If you find yourself making excuses for people, you become low-hanging fruit for a bully. Recognise this easily fixable weak spot at your core.

People-pleasers live a sad and frustrating existence with their exploiters placing huge demands on them and treating them with contempt and ingratitude. And you know what? People don't treat us well when we don't treat ourselves well. If you are a people-pleaser, check the signals you are sending out.

How to strengthen your core spirit

Here's one way of treating yourself well. You know what you like and you definitely know what you dislike, so you must set boundaries by letting people know what you will and will not do. Speak up and say what is important to you. You can say it softly, or you can say it loudly, but you must say it firmly.

Be alert when people talk you into things you are not ready for. The more you allow it, the more they do it and you find yourself getting tense and unhappy. Recognise that you are unhappy and learn to say 'no' to people. It becomes easy when you begin saying 'no' to yourself when you find you are doing something you don't want to.

When you are stuck with a nitpicking, offensive prick

Mutual respect is a must for any successful relationship. In a live-in relationship or marriage, fighting and squabbling over every little thing dwindles into something like sibling rivalry. If you wanted to spend the greater part of your life doing that, you need not have left your parents' house in the first place. This is worse because this is not a sibling relationship of your early youth, this is adult life.

For a start, you don't have to stay in destructive conversations. Change the topic. If they ignore your attempts to talk about something else, walk away. Remove yourself from any situation where you are being bullied. Sometimes you find yourself committed to a bully who knows your boundaries but refuses to respect them. You must distance yourself from the bully. If you feel overwhelmed, or if it just doesn't feel right, don't make a big deal out of it. Just say 'no' and change the subject.

Before you respect, honour and care for others, the sensible thing to do is to respect, honour and care for yourself.

The covert bully

Sometimes the disrespect is covert. Your partner will resort to sarcasm or round-about insults indirectly aimed at you. With the passive-aggressive, you can't quite put your finger on it but you feel off-balance most of the time. You ask them if they are okay, but instead of coming out with what's biting them, they say that everything is just fine.

They insult you even while offering you congratulations on a promotion or a successful assignment. Sometimes they ignore your good fortune entirely or they take offense at something you say and give you the silent treatment. Sometimes they agree to a certain action and then renege on it. They insult you and gloat over your discomfiture. They love that you feel hurt, because that was intended, but they will insist that they did nothing to hurt you.

The covert bully to my mind is as bad as the overt bully, sometimes worse. The only solution is to call them out on the insult. Don't accept it and nurse your hurt, because not only are you playing into their hands, you are hurting yourself and your personal growth.

Ask them a direct question and do not settle for anything other than a direct answer. If you want them shaken and stirred, try saying this to your bully: 'Something's bugging you. Let's talk about that now, because what you just said, hurt me.'

Exploitative people don't like anyone they exploit; what they like is exploiting you and others like you. Pleasing exploitative people so that they like you is wrong. What is right is that *you* like you.

It is important to communicate clearly that you don't like the sneaky insults or the sneaky put-downs. Don't get sucked into the drama. Don't fight fire with fire. Don't retaliate by being passive-aggressive in turn. That passive aggressiveness will not go away because it is a character trait and the constant erosion of your self-respect will continue. If you can compartmentalise and rise above it, stay. If you cannot, then walk away.

Serena's story

This very calm woman, Serena (well, yes, name changed), lives in my neighbourhood. She is soft-spoken and calm but one fine afternoon, there she was screaming at her husband, who is the neighbourhood creep.

'I HAVE HAD A LOT OF PATIENCE WITH YOU. NOW THAT IS AT AN END!' She told him he could leave, get OUT! He told her it was his house so she should 'Jes' fuck off'. She's seventy years old. Know what I'm saying? She's seventy. That is not the situation you want to find yourself in when you are seventy years old.

Serena's husband, aka El Creepo, insulted her and spoke provocative nonsense whenever friends or family visited her. Serena, like so many of us, decided it was best to ignore his behaviour. He had been talking down to her since they married. And his conduct just grew more outrageous and offensive as the years passed.

The error she made, like a large number of the rest of us, both men and women, was to allow the first incident of disrespect to go unchallenged. She should have in that instant told him that she would not tolerate it. Not ten, twenty or fifty years later.

Don't let it happen to you, my friend. You have a foot. Put your foot down the first time he disrespects you. Or plant it on his ass and kick him out of your life.

When you do it, do it with elegance. No hemming or hawing. No stuttering or stammering. Above all, please, no weeping or screaming or trembling lips. Look directly into his eyes and tell him to stop disrespecting you and to stop that right now. You must do this the very first time it happens. Listen to me. I'm old, I'm wise and I *KNOW* this shit.

It's all in the voice. A curt level tone telling him that you are equal partners and if he is going to disrespect you, he might as well leave right now. Or you lean forward slightly, stare into your bully's eyes and then issue a threat in a cold, clear voice. Or you mix a strong laxative in his meal. Joking, just joking.

Serena's retirement into hurt silence the first time her husband disrespected her, became a way of life for her. His bullying and general obnoxiousness became a way of life for him. That is the kiss of death in any relationship—not just marriage. If the other person has no respect for you, what is the point? Walk away, or tell them to leave. Who knew they would hate each other at a time when two elderly people need each other's companionship?

Old age is a time in your life to spend with someone whom you have travelled the miles together. Someone you enjoy being with, someone you can talk to and someone you can eat, sleep, burp and fart with and feel no embarrassment. Someone you are so comfortable with, you don't mind the stupid things he does and he doesn't mind the stupid things you do. That is love. That is the deep, growing, lasting kind of love. Complete ease in each other's company.

Let me tell you, the early years just fly past. Before you know it, you are old. And those senior years can be a major pain if you are living with a partner you don't really like. You continue living together in a slow boil resenting each other, because there is nowhere else either of you can go. That is no way to live. Life is whole when you actually love the person you are living with.

Own your space

It takes self-awareness of knowing who you are and telling your partner who you are. It is the practical thing to do and becomes a turning point in your relationship where you lay down ground rules. That's how you own your space and ensure you're not pushed around. That goes for the spouse, kids, colleagues and the man or woman on the street. Don't make excuses for disrespect towards you. Never allow an insult to go unchallenged. If it upsets you, challenge it.

In the beginning a relationship is a shining shapeless thing. Both parties are doing their best to make the other feel they are the luckiest people in the world. After a while someone sets the rules in the relationship and takes over. If either one of you turns out to be a bully or a control freak, then that is not a good situation—for you or for him.

There's no Mr or Ms Perfect. When we meet anyone, we place our best self forward. You quickly figure out what he likes and mould yourself according to that. He quickly figures out what you are looking for and slips into that character role just for you. The genuine article is often quite different. Happens all the time. We market ourselves to each other, and neither is quite aware of what the other is truly like.

It's like buying a pig in a poke. Back in the day, people used to sell pigs by putting one in a bag they called a 'poke'. More often than not, the buyer of the pig would find a skinny pig, or a cat or a dog in the poke and the buyer who did not check was conned. (Bet you thought it meant getting a pig who is only interested in poking you. Since the beginning of Time, that's uppermost in the average guy's mind. Not that that would be a bad thing—if getting poked was uppermost in your mind too.)

You don't get a fair idea of what Mr Right is all about until you have lived with him for six months. If you want the true picture, wait until the kids come. That's when the guy's real character emerges. Yours too, for that matter.

It is not worth the misery of continuing with someone who treats you with disrespect. If you can leave, do so. If you cannot, because you have responsibilities or nowhere else to go, then set about barricading yourself emotionally. Compartmentalise your bully in your mind and your space so that he does not destroy the quality of your life outside of him. Catch up with friends and family, get a hobby or pursue a long-forgotten passion.

Any addiction can destroy you, even love

There are those who are so desperately in love that they become willing victims for as long as their bullies can feed on their distress. The bullying is like the sting of the needle to a heroin addict, something that gives you pain. But after that, the sheer high his attention gives you makes you accept the pain as par for the course. Any battered woman will tell you the initial addiction to their bully blinded them to early signs of violence.

If your relationship is an addiction, recognise it and stop it there and then. If you do not, one bleak day you will realise the highs have gone and it is only the bullying that continues.

Serena made excuses saying all men are bastards. No. They're not. Most men are nice bastards. You just have to look out for the signs that show up the real monsters. You owe it to yourself to recognise them. They manifest in the beginning of your relationship in ways that destroy your sense of self-worth.

In the next two chapters, we will be discussing mental abuse and domestic violence. You will then understand why it is imperative that you stop disrespect in its tracks, or if you cannot, why you must break off a toxic relationship.

3

Mental Abuse and How to Deal With It

Have you reached a stage where it is impossible to have a normal conversation without being insulted or shouted at? Does he look like he is enjoying himself when he insults you? Are you always on edge?

Disrespect is one thing. That can be sorted out at the beginning of the relationship, but mental abuse is a whole different can of worms. Disrespect can be the early signs of a toxic individual. But often it can be merely careless speech or actions, which can be stopped. A toxic individual, for instance, a malignant narcissist or a violent bully, does not show any disrespect in the beginning of a relationship. They woo you with skill. They sweep you off your feet. The bullying begins slowly as they push boundaries and test your levels of acceptance, until one terrible day you realise that the partner you are so committed to behaves like he should be locked up in a prison. If he is angry all the time, accusing you of things you never did, unable to have a normal conversation without insulting you, your bully could be suffering from Narcissistic Personality Disorder.

We often make the mistake of thinking our permanently angry partner is in some kind of angry depression. We think we've done something wrong and for the life of us cannot figure out why there is so much contempt, resentment, if not open hatred, towards us. We hope things will sort themselves out, but I can tell you from sorry experience, they don't.

This partner or spouse who subjects you to mental abuse used to be a completely different, supposedly happy, person in the beginning of the relationship. Gradually this weird personality trait takes over. If not controlled, your bully develops into what is called a Malignant Narcissist. And you never see it coming. It's like you are swimming in cool, calm, emerald waters and suddenly you find yourself jerked off your feet by this riptide.

A bully and a riptide have the same endgame

Now the thing with a riptide is this. If you struggle and fight it, you tire yourself out and the riptide will drag you out of your depth and drown you. The riptide is a strong current that is shaped like a head and shoulders in the water and since it runs perpendicular to the shoreline, it comes flowing swiftly to the shore and pulls whatever is in its path out to sea. While every instinct of yours has you fighting it and trying to swim to the shore, you don't fight a riptide. You *never* fight a riptide, just like you never fight a malignant narcissist.

Ignore your instinct to fight free of it; instead, relax and escape it by floating or treading water parallel, not perpendicular, to the shore. You do this slowly and calmly, conserving your energy until you get out from the far end of the current, past the head and past the shoulder, and then you swim to the shore, once the pull disappears. And you savour that heady taste of freedom.

See? You've learned how to save yourself at sea and *also* how to handle your bully. It's the same technique. Once you know that a riptide can rob you of life as you know it, you don't let it pull you down. You don't struggle. You don't fight it. You float above it. You distance yourself from it. You treat your bully the very same way. You know he's there, so you go about your business keeping an eye on him but living life the way you want to. The riptide ends up looking like a complete fool.

According to experts like Dr Ramani Durvasula, clinical psychologist and author of the book, *Should I Stay or Should I Go: Surviving a Relationship with a Narcissist,* 20 to 30 percent of humans suffer from Narcissistic Personality Disorder (NPD). These are human riptides whose sole purpose in life seems to drag you down and destroy you.

You make the mistake of thinking they are in a depression that will go away with love and kindness. You could actually be enabling the narcissistic disorder into full-blown malignancy.

What you think is not rocking the boat is actually enabling the disorder.

You get sucked into struggling 24×7 through the decades keeping the peace. Or, having blistering quarrels you can never win, fighting back the panic and swallowing your despair.

While researching this chapter, I learned that there are men and a growing number of women who use words to maim and destroy the self-worth of those who love and depend on them for support. It could be spouses, parents, family members, employers, co-workers, friends, siblings—malignant narcissists are everywhere and they affect the quality of life of millions.

Malignant narcs don't lift a hand against you, but they are more common than wife beaters. They reduce their victims to abject slavery through sustained emotional abuse. Mental health professionals call this Malignant Narcissism.

The research says that this personality trait, Narcissistic Personality Disorder, affects both men and women who have had an unbalanced childhood. When he was a child, a malignant narc's parents ignored his emotional needs. They were very proud and caring of him in the public eye but paid no attention to him in the confines of the home. Sometimes one of the narc's parents was very cold or harsh with him while the other was very lenient. This unbalanced parenting usually guarantees supplying the world with a malignant narc. It is not all bad though.

Narcs make excellent corporate bosses, heads of organisations and successful politicians; they are excellent judges of character and brilliant users of people. But they are unhappy people, quite rotten within, and those around them shrivel and die inside.

The internet is full of recognised experts on, and survivors of, narcissism. It is an ongoing process where one person systematically diminishes, then destroys the inner life and mental balance of another. Here are some of the signs of the narc gathered from the internet, friends and personal experience.

Continuous criticism is the first sign

The bully you are with wants you to fail. Understand that he is never going to acknowledge your successes and will always treat you like a piece of dirt. He will criticise you constantly but he will go berserk when he is criticised. Entertainment and joy become an anathema to him where you are concerned. There will be no celebrations, no greetings, no movies, or theatre, or even walks in the park. Anything that makes you happy, or indeed that makes any normal person happy, will be vetoed on the spot.

Gaslighting in every conversation

You cannot have a normal calm conversation with a malignant narcissist. Conversations with your narc disorient you and make you question your reality to the point when you begin doubting yourself. He or she will distort facts and worse, repeat the same distorted lies over and over again. This is called 'gaslighting'. You feel confused and frustrated.

You often tell yourself you should have recorded an earlier conversation that he is now denying. That is the minute you decide whether he is just forgetful or whether you are in a relationship with a person with NPD. If he is a malignant narcissist, then reconsider staying, because time will only make him worse.

Always negative, difficult conversations and self-praise

He's a complete drag to listen to. Far from sparkling conversation, the general thread of his conversation will always be shallow and full of negativity, zeroing in on politics, bad weather, tragedies, conflicts, disease, gossip, rumours, who died, who's dying, who deserves punishment, who is out to get him and generally, how the world is going to hell in a hand-basket. He will always hold the moral high ground and regularly brag and broadcast evidence of his superiority among men. He will also remind you of how he overcame a history of losses and catastrophes in his life when things went horribly wrong. He will repeat stories of how he triumphed despite them or how everyone else is to blame for his failures, if any, but never he.

Narcs have double standards

Abusers have different rules for themselves and different rules for their victims. They will criticise anyone even if they know jack about the subject under discussion. When questioned they will bluster that they could have done a better job, were it up to them.

Mentally healthy people do not belittle others constantly. Abusers want the whole world to be perfect, but their minds are a complete mess. The subject of their conversation when it is not criticising you is that what everyone else is doing is wrong.

They do not love anyone, they only pretend to

By definition the narcissist is completely in love with himself. He has nothing left for you or anyone else. He needs to possess, to control, to own the other person. He can only mimic physical demonstrations of love in the beginning of your relationship to lure you, but you will never feel a genuine connection because a malignant narcissist cannot reciprocate. His conversation will be devoid of love or empathy or consideration for anyone else. If you mention someone else's plight, he will shrug it off as something the person deserved.

You always feel the need to apologise and you don't know why

Victims of narcs feel an overwhelming need to apologise, because they feel they must have done something that is setting the narc off. Narcissists will not settle for a mere apology; they require that you grovel. They won't ever apologise for their behaviour. You put up with this nonsense because you think it has to be your fault but you don't know what you have done to bring on all this resentment. You decide that he is suffering from some kind of depression. That's a serious mistake. It is not depression. What he is inflicting on you is mental abuse.

No sense of humour

Even though they laugh a lot when at a social event, they laugh when they think they are expected to laugh. The malignant narcissist has no sense of humour because they are rotten inside (Dr Ramani's words, not mine, but I second them). They fail often and they cannot handle failure because they live in fear of failure, so that's another spiral they are trapped in. It is there in every conversation you have, and every conversation feels more like an examination when you are probed for information that will be used against you for future torture.

If you turn the conversation towards neutral mundane topics, your narc will be dismissive and irritated because he has a very limited attention span if the theme of the conversation is not focused on him.

He is always spoiling for a fight

Every conversation will quickly spiral into a scream fest with him disagreeing, ranting and trying to pick fights. Watch how hypersensitive and jealous your narc gets. He will take what you offer in the conversation, bounce it for a bit, and then pick a molehill and turn it into a mountain in seconds.

He will look for reasons to be insulted and if he cannot find them, he will just make them up so that everything is your fault and his outrage is justified. When he finishes bawling you out for some imagined insult, you will notice a look of sadistic satisfaction and contempt on his face.

If you have an opinion that contradicts his, get ready for

a full-fledged attack. Abusers have very low self-esteem and he will overreact to little things like jokes and unimportant issues. Narcs take every opinion contrary to theirs as a personal insult.

The fault is never his; the blame is always yours

An early sign of a narc is that he always takes credit for something that turns out well but always blames others when things go bad. Even in the case of his own failures, the narc will always blame others but you will be the one who is blamed permanently.

Narcs never come forth with a genuine apology

Do not ever expect an apology from a malignant narcissist. Even if they are caught out in a lie, or a mistake, they will never admit they are at fault. If anything goes wrong, the abuser will blame others and force others to agree with them. This means that expecting an apology from your abuser is almost impossible. He will apologise only if it is in his interest, but the apology will never be genuine.

He is vicious towards your friends and family

Your narc will reserve special venom for those you are close to. He will criticise and question your closest friends and family without feeling bad or guilty about his hurtful words. He will make you feel guilty for spending time with those you love and find comfort with.

He is perfectly normal with strangers and chance acquaintances

That's your domestic reality. Outside he is completely different—he can be very entertaining and extremely charming. You know it is just pretence so that he can maintain his public image. He appears to be kind and attentive to those he meets, but you know that he is flat out evil in the privacy of your home. If he does joke at home, it will be to make inappropriate jokes at your expense. The only time he smiles is when he is mocking you. He seems oblivious to causing you distress and he shows no regret or awareness that he has crossed the line. But understand this: he feeds on your distress and grows strong.

You find you have two lives—one external and visible to the outside world and the other internal and unseen. Your life is ruined by a bully who never puts his hands on you. He uses the same systems as the wife-batterer to cut off your financial, familial, social and emotional independence, but he does not lay a hand on you.

A malignant narcissist only gets worse with age

Mental health professionals advise you to leave a narc, but sometimes you cannot. Maybe you are too old. Maybe you have nowhere else to go. Maybe you are an enabler who takes the abuse and makes excuses for his behaviour; an empath who feels she can change him because love will conquer all.

You fear him, yet you convince yourself that you love him and that deep down under all that rage, he loves you too. Maybe you need him in your life. Maybe despite everything else, you both work well together, because a narc is highly intelligent and capable of quick thinking in emergencies. They are very afraid of death and take great care to remain safe and in good health. In that case, you need to keep watertight boundaries when dealing with a narc.

Those were the signs of a malignant narcissist. Now here are a few simple tips to get back your equilibrium. Really simple tips.

Accept that you are in an abusive relationship

Mental torture is abuse. If your partner constantly puts you down, especially in front of others; if he is extremely jealous; if he loses his temper easily; if he tries to keep you away from friends and family; if he has unrealistic expectations of you; if friends or family members warned you about this person—if these ifs are your reality, then you are a victim or a survivor of mental abuse.

How to handle a narc if you cannot dump him

The first step is to manage your expectations so you don't get your heart broken over and over again. If you think you need to be patient and you will get him to love you again, understand that narcs, by definition, never love anyone except themselves. Remember, Narcissus fell in love with his reflection in the pond and he fell in and drowned.

Your narc never loved you because he was and is incapable of love. The moment you accept that fact is when your healing begins. Look inward and you will feel an awareness of freedom that increases every day. The establishment can help you with a violent partner, but mental abuse from a malignant narcissist is impossible to fight in courts. However, experts say it can be tackled and kept under control.

Treat your narc as you would a toddler throwing a tantrum

Essentially the malignant narc has the same attitude as a four-year-old toddler prone to throwing temper tantrums at the drop of a hat. You cannot reason with a tantrum-throwing toddler. You cannot hug and kiss his rage away. You need to find the toddler's chink and issue a threat you have no qualms about carrying out. The best way is to present your opinion, respond to the backlash, but do not react. Be calm, be tranquil, be interested in something else.

Compartmentalise your narc

Put him in a compartment in your life; do not let him interfere or get involved in your profession or your mental space. The narc cannot change his personality; he may try to change it for a while but will lapse back. You, who are the victim of the narc, must keep facts and witnesses on call. You must not be a martyr. You keep enduring abuse, you keep enduring rage and you keep enduring having your reality tested on a regular basis. Stop that.

Avoid engaging with your abuser

Spend as little time alone with your abuser as is possible. Surround yourself with friends and family who are closer to you than he. Have them check on you periodically and always let them know where you are going. Take all the emotional comfort and support you can from those who care about you.

Respond, never react

The narc thrives on supply that he gets from a reaction of rage or distress from you. He will lob a provocative comment into the conversation and you have to be alert to respond but not react. That is all it takes! If you react, he counters with insult and abuse in a matter of seconds.

When you react with insult or abuse in turn, or dissolve into tears, or try to reason with him, you end up feeding his disorder. This is called giving the narc 'supply'. That only escalates the verbal assault. He thrives on it while something dies inside of you. So respond, do not react. Be calm, be tranquil, be vague and leave that negative space if you cannot walk out of the relationship. You have to starve the narc of supply.

If you can do so, you must leave

No one deserves a life like this; everyone deserves to be safe. By his words and actions, your partner will show that he knows more about you than you do about yourself and your life. This will increase as time goes by until you lose sight of who you are. He sets roles for you as a couple, and if those roles don't sit well with you, he shows his displeasure. You must be immune from his displeasure. Do not react. Respond as you will to a screaming toddler. Be calm, be tranquil and busy yourself with something else. Starve him of supply.

If you are going to dump him, have a proper plan

Plan a safe breakup. Tell people close to you that you are planning to get out of the relationship and that you will need their help in the coming weeks.

Next, figure out how you will deliver the news. If you are afraid of your abuser's reaction, take someone with you.

Keep the breakup conversation short. Say you are leaving and why. It is your decision, not his, so do not drag it out with excuses and reasons and apologies. Above all give no apology. Then leave.

Go and do something that makes you feel healthy and happy with the people you are comfortable with. Catch up with people who will help you stand on your own feet. You don't have to be alone.

Mental torture or any kind of bullying begins with one incident of disrespect. The solution is to nip it in the bud immediately. Zero tolerance for disrespect must be your mantra, regardless of what the situation may be. No excuses, especially if you are desperately in love with your bully.

Seeing any of these signs once or twice doesn't establish the character of an abuser. The individual is an abuser when these incidents happen regularly. Be wise, trust your instincts, and if something doesn't feel right, be on your guard. You will feel confused with the mixed signals from your abuser in the beginning of your relationship when he will alternate between nasty and nice.

He says he loves you but you wake up every morning nervous and spend the day like you are walking on eggs. You know he plays mind games with you and changes the rules constantly. Everything you do makes him angry and he is beginning to scare you.

Do not make excuses for him. Find a way to escape or deal with him by isolating him in your mind and in your life. Understand that you cannot fix the bastard's emotional problems because they are caused by a mess in his wiring, not in yours.

This is not one woman's story, or one victim's story, or your story or mine. This is a common and identical story, happening to too many women today. It's happening to men too.

A friend who read this chapter wrote that she felt like vomiting after every paragraph because her story was identical. A woman I travelled with on an overnight train journey found that her husband whom she left at age sixty-two had every one of these characteristics.

The most difficult part of your repair process is to accept that he never ever loved you. It had nothing to do with you. He is just incapable of loving anyone other than himself. Once you understand and accept that fact, you are home free.

4

Domestic Violence—Do Not Wait for the Second Assault

Are you afraid of your lover or spouse? Does he threaten to use violence on you? Has he already assaulted you? Has he isolated you from family, friends and your regular support systems?

Over the decades, reading the headlines, studying police statistics, writing reports, listening to people, seeing beaten women, I wondered, why is it second nature for so many men to disparage women? It makes no sense to hate half your species on principle, just because they are women. Where does this deep-rooted resentment for women come from? I have given this much thought and my conclusion is this. Men who give women the stink-eye resent or hate two things about women—their minds and their vaginas.

Think about it. A woman who can think for herself and say yes to most things but no to some things drives certain men into paroxysms of rage. The vagina, I think, is the crux. Certain men punish women with sex, either with sexual assault or they scurry around penis in hand ready to cheat, looking for other vaginas. Or they accuse their women of being 'whores'. And why do so many men use the phrase, 'All you do is lie back and spread your legs'?

Something in their DNA hates the fact that the woman can use her vagina to take into her body something as pissy and messy as a man's semen, perform some magic within and create Life. A small human being in her image or the semen provider's image is created. That's what certain toxic men cannot handle. There are so many of them. My second question is why do women tolerate this?

For reasons unknown, too many women fall desperately in love with men who hate women. Yes, hate. Only hatred can result in a man smashing his fist into his wife or girlfriend's face, or flinging her across a room, or breaking her bones. Domestic violence is real and happening all around us.

How it begins and grows

'There is a common pattern of behaviour followed by abusers, which is meant to control the woman in order to change her sense of self, her identity, her behaviour, which the male batterer cannot tolerate,' says Bernardo Villafañe, licenced clinical social worker (LCSW) and therapist, who deals with male domestic violence abusers. It begins gradually, he says. First comes the charm when he sweeps her off her feet, and then the controls are set in place. She doesn't notice at first and goes along with the controls.

'Domestic violence begins with the words "shut up,"' says Villafañe, 'then it escalates to five forms of abuse—emotional abuse, psychological abuse, sexual abuse, economic abuse and of course, physical abuse.'

You, who have not been touched by it, will question her staying, if she is getting beaten time after time. It's because she is in desperate love with her bully. She fears losing him even more than she fears him.

When your brain settles into freeze mode

There are situations in life when the brain sends the body into flight-or-fight mode. An individual under attack from a random stranger will stay and fight, or flee the scene immediately.

With domestic violence at the hands of a trusted, loved partner, a third F controls your brain and your body. It is the freeze mode. Your brain shuts down and you cannot think. It does not send out any fight-or-flight signals. It just freezes. With domestic violence, you are immobile and you just wait for the pain to end.

If at this point you are thinking, 'It will never happen to me. I will never allow anyone to control me,' let me tell you that no one knowingly dives into an abusive relationship. Men who are violent towards women and children are two types—the openly aggressive and the smooth charmer. You can easily avoid an aggressive character, but beware the smooth charmer.

Abusive relationships don't just happen; there are clear signs and those relationships are avoidable. Abusers select a target and they use a certain pattern of tactics to get what they want.

Violent partners show signs early in the relationship and you can gracefully bow out. Here it is important to know that all men are not ticking time bombs. The majority are perfectly normal; they will have other problems surely (who doesn't?) but they will draw the line at assaulting women and children.

Recognise the early signs of a predator

Author of '*Crazy Love*', domestic-abuse survivor Leslie Morgan Steiner, says an abuser will make you feel so loved and so passionate about him, you won't know he is controlling you as you relinquish your life to him, a minute at a time. You go weak at the knees when you find that you are his chosen one. He takes up residence in your heart, in your actions and in your mind. He is steady and solid. One thing you know in your bones is that he is a really nice guy. It's only later when he breaks those same bones that you know you made a grave error of judgement.

He was physically strong too and that was so thrilling because he was adorably gentle with you. Such gentleness from such strength added to the desperate love you have for him. You cannot believe how lucky you are. Until you realise that your luck ran out the day you locked eyes with him.

Like an expert angler, he reels you in using seduction and charm. You open your life to him and he walks in and begins the takeover in earnest. It's that simple for him. And you don't have a clue because you are falling deeply, desperately in love. There is no hint of violence or control in the beginning.

The charmer will do a few nice things for you but will leave you in no doubt that he aims to take control of your appearance, your friendships, your time, your thoughts, your decisions, your life. Study the charmer carefully; if he shows no empathy for anyone other than himself, if he flies into a fury when he does not get his way, or is not taken seriously, leave him. As your relationship deepens, you will find that this individual inserting himself into your life will show no feelings of compassion, no emotional attachment and scariest of all, he will have no feelings of guilt.

Grooming, manipulation, control

Domestic-abuse survivors say that domestic abusers employ early tactics called 'grooming'. Grooming is carefully planned behaviour saying and doing things to lure a person in. Then comes the manipulation stage when they inspire your trust, intensifying your emotional attachment and they increase control over everything you do.

Too much of charm and protestations of love

They follow a pattern. You need to stop and think when they turn on the charm. There will be too much charm, loads of compliments, so many gifts, too much togetherness, continuous talk about a shared future and too many promises. The abuser sweeps you off your feet. You feel thrilled and overwhelmed.

That's your warning signal. Take a step back. Dust off your Bullshit Radar and pay heed.

The relationship moves really fast. Within a few days or weeks of knowing you, he begins referring to you as his girlfriend, or his future wife, or he actually lays claim to you saying, 'You are mine now.' He makes plans for the both of you; he wants to move in with you, or marry you and you don't even know each other yet.

Your transformation

Then he tries to transform you. He gives you unsolicited advice and comments on your appearance and on your taste, your beliefs, your career and your personal style. A regular comment from him would be, 'You know what you need to do?'

You are thrilled that you have someone who loves you so deeply that he is hyper possessive and so jealous of the people you spend time with. That glee would be an error on your part.

Real love does not need or demand controlling rights over your life. Real love gives you freedom and room to grow as individuals so that you can grow together as a unit. The bottom line is this: you never walk on eggs around real love. You will find that you are never really comfortable with a potential abuser. Your sixth sense kicks in and sends out warning signals, which, of course, you ignore.

Removal of potential witnesses from your life

Another sign of abusers is that they don't like witnesses. They like to control their environment and thrive in isolation. The predator first begins to isolate you from those you are close to. He will set about ruining your relationships with your family and friends.

He will be upset and unsociable when family and friends visit. He will criticise them and start questioning their motives. And since you are so deep under his spell, you will think maybe he is correct in his assumptions. You begin avoiding contact with your family and friends.

He will convince you that he is the only person who really gets you. He will say it is you two together against the world. You feel so special that you don't question why the two of you even *need* to be against the world.

You are drawn in so skilfully that you miss what is happening, and it works. Predators will lie and deceive to achieve total control. Your only protection, and defence, is to get away from the person controlling you.

Control begins with the small things

He will always decide where and when you will meet. He will decide where to sit and what you should eat. You allow this because you want him to like you and you want him to think that you are easy-going. In a short time, he will be issuing orders and you will just obey.

Gaining your trust with the late-night chats

He wants more. He wants your complete trust. He wants you to fall deeply, desperately in love with him. He will find ways and means to occupy your time and keep tabs on you. He will spend time with you or message you or call you, mostly on video calls so he knows where you are at all times of the day. He will turn up at your place of work or home and escort you wherever you need to go. He will collect you too.

It would be a mistake to feel protected. He will talk into the night, and this late-night attention he showers on you creates an artificial intimacy. It is as if you have known him for a long time. You will trust him and think you are soulmates and you end up sharing personal details you probably wouldn't share in the cold light of day. The predator stores these nuggets of information away very carefully for later use.

Thought control is next

He will try to convince you of his views on issues. At this time, he will show annoyance at you deciding things for yourself. He will try to change your mind, and if you observe carefully, you will see the anger simmering under the surface if your point of view differs from his. This should warn you to back off from that relationship because before long that rage will bubble up to the surface.

He will keep you off-balance

Remember those confidences you shared with him when you were feeling relaxed and vulnerable? He will use them to manipulate you. He will pick on your every flaw and mistake, keeping you always nervous and self-conscious around him. He will make you feel unintelligent and unattractive. You will start to pull away, because you are hurt and humiliated, and he will immediately relent and treat you like someone special again. This combination of nice and nasty creates an unhealthy bond between the two of you. This bond is strong, much stronger than if he were uniformly mildly nice to you all along, because you are desperate to cling to your belief that he loves you with the same intensity that you love him.

Your first red flag is the way you make excuses for him

You make excuses and rationalise the abuser's actions and you miss the red flags. In truth, making excuses for him should be your brightest red flag. You have no idea of the danger you are in. Even when they can see the warning signs of a violent person, women find it hard to say no. They don't want to upset their lover.

Sometimes your family and friends let you down. You sense something that bothers you and you consult your well-meaning friends and family but they tell you that you are imagining things and not to let go of him. They tell you to give him another chance and to have a little patience. Listen to your gut instinct. If you know that you feel fearful about annoying him, end the relationship before it gets serious. The longer you wait, the more difficult it gets to escape from an abusive relationship.

Abusers believe that you have no right to refuse

You are an object to them. Usually the abuser just ignores your rejection. He will use every trick in the book to keep himself in your life and you under his control. He is skilled in the art of the nice and nasty. You will have one or two good days of charm and attention, followed by three or four bad days of constant insult, fighting and sullen silences. That becomes your normal. You have to be strong enough to withstand the pressure he is mounting. Understand that this person is ultimately trying to ruin your life.

Young women are most vulnerable

Domestic violence crosses all ages, race, class and creed. Leslie Morgan Steiner states that women between the ages of sixteen and twenty-four are believed to be three times more likely to experience domestic abuse than any other age group. She spoke in the context of the United States of America. But it holds true across the world. These are the years we are most vulnerable to falling desperately in love. One continues to make excuses for his rage, but now you know that you are afraid of him.

He may decide to take you away from the place you call home to a new district or country, far away from all your support systems.

Sometimes, yes, adventurous couples like getting away and striking out on their own. Both partners look at it as an adventure. If there is no sign of your spouse being a control freak, micromanaging your life and threatening violence if you object to it, then you have nothing to worry about.

A victim does not suspect that her predator is isolating her so that he can begin beating her into total submission. You are not paranoid. You agree to move away from your support systems and maybe a job that you love because you love him desperately and will do whatever he wants to make him happy. You push your own needs under the carpet and do what is best for him, even though it means leaving friends and family.

Battered victims in their testimonies said they never suspected they were moved out of their comfort zones to a place where neighbours wouldn't know them well enough to come to protect them. They had no family or close relatives around. The woman usually had no job and colleagues to confide in. There will be no one, they said, to take note of their bruises and fractures.

If this is happening to you, he now has you physically under his control with no help at hand. He has you financially under his control since you don't have a job anymore or have no control over your bank account. He has you psychologically under his control since you are desperately in love with him with no way out and therefore desperate to make him happy no matter what. But the first blow has not yet struck you. He is building up to that. First, he must set his controls in place: physical, financial and psychological.

He introduces the threat of violence

Maybe he steps up menacingly, or raises a hand or shoves you to see how you will react. Maybe he breaks things you love or throws things to show his displeasure. Or uses words of violence and states that he will hit you the next time you cross the line with him. You must react now. Your sanity and your life depend on it.

When the first threat of violence is issued, do not ignore it or make excuses for his temper, or frustration, or any stupid justification that enters your love-addled brain. You have to recognise that you are in danger and deal with it.

Tell him clearly and calmly that you will retaliate, that you will inform the cops, your neighbours, your family and your friends. Tell him if he raises a hand on you, you will go to the local media and the police and spread the word. Do not quail. Do not tremble. Head back to your familiar background, head back to your family, get your old job back or get another job.

If you don't put your foot down at the first threat of violence, he *will* assault you, make no mistake of that. Far from being your husband or your lover, he is the enemy. At that time, you will accept that you are living with the enemy and that the enemy is a monster. He is an implacable foe with no sense of guilt or remorse, and he can kill you. If he hits you once and gets away with it, he will hit you again and again.

After the first beating

After it happens the first time, he will be touchingly contrite. He will apologise and beg forgiveness and swear that he would rather cut off his arm before he raises a hand on you a second time. If you believe him and forgive him and put this behind you as a one-off because he was having a bad day, and you are convinced that you brought it upon yourself, you are putting yourself in grave danger. The next time he beats you, he will say it is your fault because you are forcing him to beat you.

Once he falls into a pattern of beating you and blaming you, then you will fall into a pattern of taking the beatings and blaming yourself.

Your window of opportunity to escape was wide open when he issued the threat of violence the very first time. That window was still open the first time he resorted to violence. Once you forgive the first beating, make excuses for it and choose to continue living with him, and tolerate subsequent beatings, that window of opportunity is shut. He will not allow you to leave because he feeds off the beatings. He also feeds off your terror, your pain and your misery between the beatings.

You will be in equally great danger if you try to leave now with no protection or support systems you can turn to for help. If you read reports on domestic violence, you will learn that most domestic-violence murders happen after the victim has physically escaped from her abuser. Death of his victim is the final high for the psychotic abuser.

His level of entitlement makes it clear that he owns you, that you are his property, and if he can't have you, no one else can.

Activities outside the relationship will be completely banned. He wants complete capitulation from you in everything he demands; any refusal results in punishment, withdrawal of love; and violence. Do not wait for concrete evidence of risk. If you feel afraid, there's a good reason why you are feeling this way.

Understand the signs when you are in danger of being killed

- The physical violence increases in severity and frequency.
- You stifle thoughts that your partner is capable of killing you.
- Your partner has attempted to choke you, essentially broadcasting his ability to kill.
- He owns a gun.
- He has given you injuries in the past that could have resulted in your death.
- He was violent towards you when you were pregnant.
- He controls all your activities.
- He threatens you with a weapon.
- He forces you to have sex.
- He uses street drugs or is a problem drinker.
- He has threatened to kill you and then kill himself.
- He becomes unemployed and feels worthless and angry.
- He experiences any traumatic event or receives proof that the relationship is over.
- He is violent towards your children.
- He is violent outside of the home and destroys things that are important to you.

- He stalks you or has others reporting to him on your activities.

You are at risk when you threaten to leave, when you leave, and three months to a year after you leave. These are extremely high-risk periods.

How to save yourself

If you are worried that he might get violent, it is because the potential for violence is already there. The first warning sign of violence is if you have an intuitive feeling of risk. Get the support of the community around you, neighbours, work colleagues and most important of all, law enforcement.

You can escape by talking about the domestic violence you suffer to all the people you and he know. Yes, of course there are those who will say it is none of their business. They will urge you to try and work things out yourself, but there will be others who will help and protect you.

The important thing is to get the word out that he is beating you. If you don't, he gets strength from your silence and your terror and your shame. He believes he has total control over you. Take that control away by publicly calling him out on his violence.

He is sure you will not talk to anyone about your beatings. It is a shameful secret he is convinced you will not share with anyone especially if you are in a new place. No one knows you because he has kept people from getting too close to you. You must start speaking to others now.

Create a support network of neighbours and friends

Breaking your silence may help save your life. You must spread the word sufficiently and make an official police complaint. That could scare him, or it may enrage him further because not all bullies and wife-beaters are cowards. Some are psychopaths who feel no remorse and no guilt. But you have to take the risk. Some bullies will look on you as prey to be hunted down and you will spend the rest of your life looking over your shoulder. That is no way to live.

That is why I urge you—do not allow him to isolate you from family and friends. If you have allowed him to do that, put your foot down when he issues a threat of violence. If you allow the first assault, walk away immediately. If you don't because you are so deeply in love with him, it is important to remember that there is never too deep a hole you cannot climb out of. You can always get out of an abusive relationship, but you cannot and must not do it alone. Help is out there. You just have to recognise that you need it. You have to ask for help and you have to have the strength to accept that help.

Women are taught from infancy to be sweet and gentle, quiet and obedient. When they have to actually protect themselves, they simply freeze. They tend to underestimate the danger they are in. Protect yourself any way you can. Self-defence is legal.

Meanwhile, if you are too nervous to think of self-defence, look for women's organisations in your neighbourhood that you can turn to. You must keep the number of the local police and the women's organisations on speed dial.

Immediately take pictures of the injuries you have sustained and send them to a reliable person for safekeeping. Those photographs are important evidence, not just for the complaint but to remind yourself, if or when you are tempted to fall for his contrite talk after he assaults you.

5

Surviving Dumping, Divorce or Death of a Loved One

Have you been suddenly dumped with no reason given? Has the divorce left you feeling devastated and abandoned? Has death taken away the love of your life? Do you feel an overwhelming depression?

A laughing jackass of a friend who was a success at everything he took on was completely broken when his girlfriend of five years dumped him. She told him he would not let her breathe, and it was like a light inside him had been switched off. He dragged around just going through the motions. Life happened of course and someone even better came along, but he confessed to me that he had often thought of riding his bike into oncoming traffic during that grey post-dumping period.

A friend, the kindest being you could ever find, thought the world of everyone and found someone exactly like her. They were happy and content, but ten years into the marriage, his kidneys gave out and he died. She has turned into a virtual recluse and a hoarder. She cannot bring herself to part with anything.

An acquaintance who could have written the book on how to be silly, found herself divorced when her husband fell in love with someone else and married the other woman. She is not bitter, just living in denial and complete poverty.

And I thought we humans are a weird bunch. During my agony-aunt days and over the intervening years, I learned that we can deal with almost anything, even rejection in most impersonal cases, but we cannot handle personal heartbreak. I found a few who agreed with this point of view, especially psychologist Guy Winch, author of *How to Fix A Broken Heart*, who was absolutely clear on this, so I'm sharing the observations he made during a TED talk on the same subject.

He says we can handle accidents, health challenges, academic failure, job loss, but we cannot handle heartbreak. 'This last one creates such dramatic pain that our minds tell us the cause of that pain must be dramatic too,' says Winch. This we have all experienced at some time or the other in our lives when we beat ourselves up trying to figure out what we did that was so wrong. We go down one rabbit hole after another, second-guessing our words, our actions and obsessing over every minute detail of our relationship. We cannot accept for ourselves that it just did not work out for the other partner in the relationship.

Remember that observation I made about how no two persons are equally committed to a relationship. One is a giver for most of the time, and one is a taker for most of the time. Takers generally back out of a relationship. Sometimes it is the giver who decides he or she is not getting enough out of the relationship.

The chemistry was there. He was perfect, you liked his friends and his family, he liked your family and friends, but suddenly he's up and running. You were a perfect fit but he wants out of your life and you never saw it coming.

Sometimes you are already married and it's not even five years but the cracks in your marriage are openly visible. There is no communication, no warmth, just resentment and a withdrawal into oneself. He wants a divorce, or you do, or both do.

Sometimes death separates you and dealing with life after the death of a loved one is a hard, terrible slog. How do you get up and move on once again?

You have to be willing to let go, to accept that it's over, says Guy Winch. 'Do not let your mind dwell on the "what ifs". Let go. Put it out of your mind. It's not easy recovering from a broken heart. It is exactly like recovering from an addiction. It's a fight, to make yourself whole again.'

When you are dumped and you never saw it coming

If it's desperate love, it is almost impossible to climb out of the dark hole you are hiding in. You end up being hurt twice. Once when he dumped you and the second more lingering torture you put yourself through mourning over losing him. You keep second-guessing yourself, beating yourself up wondering how, when and where you fell short.

Well, let me tell you, you didn't fall short. If he has dumped you without giving you the courtesy of a reason, then you fell hard for an idiot. But the sun will rise again tomorrow and life will go on. Is he mourning? Is he missing you? No. He's gone on like you didn't matter at all. I would ask then, why let his leaving matter to you?

His rejection came like a bolt from the blue. He won't tell you why. He won't tell you if he met anyone new. He won't tell you if it is something about you that he does not like. He gives no reason. He just says, sorry, but this is not working out. And he walks away. You will feel shock and grief, there will be anger, then depression, but there will be a day when you will find acceptance.

So let him go. You have to because he's leaving anyway. Treat him like an expensive but useless pair of shoes. You walked around in them, but they kept slipping off your feet, or turning your ankle or giving you blisters. You thought they were perfect. You paid more than you could afford to for them. But more shoes will come along, shoes that will be a more perfect fit. Return this pair immediately, or throw it in the trash and forget it.

If he does not want to be a part of your life, why would you want someone like that cluttering your space? No matter how nice a guy he is, no matter how good-looking, no matter how much physical chemistry there was between the two of you, if he does not want to be a part of your life, that's it. You turn away from him and get back to your life.

I have seen highly intelligent people fall apart after a breakup. I have seen how feeling alone and in pain has affected victims of broken hearts. It affects your health and your thinking. This affects your dealings with family and friends and your place of work. My friend, the once happy jackass, looked and behaved as if his heartbreak reduced his ability to think logically. I learned that this is true. Heartbreak breaks you.

Observing my friend and a few others over the years, heartbreak caused a deep fracture in their mental health. At least three were diagnosed with clinical depression.

I firmly believe that if someone you loved discarded you in the vilest way possible without a thought for your feelings, you must *never* dwell on the good times. It makes perfect sense to fixate instead on the bad times.

Guy Winch says pretty much the same thing. A heartbroken person should not remember the good times. He says, 'Compile an exhaustive list of all the bad points of your ex and how he was bad for you. Put it on your phone and read it every time your memory makes you yearn for all the good times you shared.'

So how do you handle heartbreak? Do not second-guess yourself; it will give you no answers. Do not allow him to waste any more of your time or your life on him. Look within yourself for validation and look around you to carry on your life as you know it.

Do not try changing yourself in any way, unless it is to look more gorgeous. This is actually a good time to pamper yourself, experiment with your looks: get a new hairstyle, new clothes, new shoes... Return to the healing power of love of family and friends. Do whatever it takes to be comfortable with who you are. Learn to trust yourself again.

Another guy may or may not come. If he arrives in your space, he may or may not be the right guy, but let people into your life who will love you and commit to you for who you are, warts and all. Hundreds, thousands, possibly millions have had their hearts broken, and have healed. You too can heal. Find your balance and find your bliss. This used to be my agony-aunt battle cry.

I know I say delete the dumper from your life, but before doing that consider getting mad and getting even. It doesn't help your misery when friends, family and colleagues keep asking you why you two had split. 'Why' would be that one question that is gnawing at your vitals.

There's this woman I knew who was so fed up with family and friends' questions that she decided to shift their attention to her ex. She smiled sadly and hinted that he was confused about his sexuality. Just a hint and of course they filled in the blanks themselves.

Her life fell apart after her boyfriend split with her. She had no idea why he dumped her after three years of seeing each other. They had exchanged engagement rings too. All he said was, 'It's just not working out for me. I feel claustrophobic.'

She was shattered, and then angry. It was worse because they lived on the same street and she saw him every day. Inquisitive friends and neighbours kept trying to find out why the golden couple had split. *She* must have done something, they said, *he* couldn't, he was such a soft and gentle soul, but what was it she did that was so terrible?

She was furious. She sighed and told random neighbours and friends, 'Well, I always suspected that you know... he was just a little... you know...? It would never have worked, so he ended it. I'm sad, but I'm really grateful to him, because I couldn't break it off.' They shook their heads and turned their attention to him, giving her the breather she so desperately needed.

Then he landed up at her door and instead of throwing ten million fits, he wrapped his arms around her and thanked her. It turned out he really was gay and did not know how to end their relationship. Now she was a saint in his eyes because 'she knew all along' and was still ready to marry him. She got the closure she needed.

Everyone's not so lucky though, so the 'dumped' must do what can be done to remove the dumper from their life. Block his number on your telephone. Delete all his photographs and all his messages. Burn any mementos you may have collected, and you will feel a lightening of spirit as you work towards closure. It's exactly like breaking an addiction—it's best to stop cold turkey.

Now you see your day like a fog before you. Earlier he was a big part of your life. So you have a choice. You can succumb to sadness, or look on this day as a time of freedom, to focus on yourself and your life. As far as you are concerned, the dumper is dead. You mourned and you raged; now it is time to get back to living your life. It is important to not let him waste any more of your time. It is important that not just mutual friends know that you are moving on, it is important that *you* know that you are moving on.

Getting back your balance after a divorce

Divorce is as final as it gets. When there are minor children to factor in, the divorce would be as traumatic, if not more, for your children, especially when they are young. There are many divorced couples who continue to have friendly relations with each other, but more often than not, divorce is a bitter and demeaning experience and very cruel on the children. If you can keep it civil, do so, for their sake. No one expected the marriage to end in divorce, but it has and there's no going back on that.

You must work on healing as thoroughly as you can. Do not stay stuck in your pain or distress. Clinical psychologist David Sbarra has simple common-sense techniques for getting back your balance. He says the first thing you have to do is get your sleep.

Sleep problems can pose serious health risks. But it is important that you get your sleep without medication. You have to train your mind to calm and tranquillity and drift into sleep.

You do this by providing compassion to yourself. Look on your pain as you would the pain of a dearly loved friend or child. Be kind to yourself. Allow your emotions to rise, allow the tears, allow the anger, but do not wallow in it.

Do not personalise your pain, says Sbarra, universalise it. So many others are going through divorce, you are not alone and you are not the only one suffering. Accept it.

Talk to people about moving on. Get back to hanging out with friends and family who enhance your sense of self-worth. Do all the things you loved doing during happier times. Focus on what you have—freedom, children, a home, good and bad memories. If you have been dumped or divorced, it's good to remember the bad times, but if you have children and you are strong enough, keep the good memories alive for their sake. Figure out ways to remove the unhappy remembrances from your life. If you can, move to a new place; if you cannot, then get rid of all the memories of your ex that hurt you. There will be pain, loneliness, questioning, but you must give yourself time to heal.

You married for several excellent reasons: happiness, bliss, joy of being in a committed relationship and raising a family. Your aim, like everybody's aim, was joy. Financial issues, health, cheating, boredom, got in the way of that joy. Let your goal of joy be non-negotiable. Give yourself time to gather your resources.

You are no longer legally bound and you know what that means, right? It means you are free. You are free to move towards that goal of joy.

The most difficult break to deal with is death

Sometimes death takes away a loved one. You never see it coming. This is more difficult to get over. The feeling of being completely alone and bereft is like an open wound that will not heal. Grief is scarily similar to fear. It makes you feel alone, terrified and isolated. Loss of a beloved spouse is something you cannot move on from. How can you? You were two parts of a whole that worked. Sometimes one tragedy comes quick on the heels of another as Life does her thing and you feel your sense of self deserting you.

After his wife died, a sixty-five-year old sibling who was so full of life, health and vitality became a shell of himself. Nothing we did could get him out of his sadness. Soon he began falling prey to all sorts of illness. They were two halves of a whole, and she died on their thirty-fifth wedding anniversary in the most tragic manner. His friends and relatives try to get him back to his earlier social life, but the difference is palpable. While in the past he was the life of the party, now he merely goes through the motions.

People tell you bracingly that you need to 'move on', that it was 'God's plan' and that 'everything happens for the best' and you want them all to die. You want to die too. When someone you deeply love dies suddenly, there is no moving on. You are bombarded by hospital officials approaching you for payment, even organ donation; you have family helping you to put away his things; you have friends telling you that you have to get title deeds and certification updated. And here you are just battling fear.

Delegate jobs to the advisors and send them packing. Keep those friends and family members who will sit quietly by you, ready to help you with the daily chores, without thrusting jobs and advice on you. Give yourself time to recover from the shock. Grieve. Allow the tears to flow. Focus gently but firmly on the good times and the wonderful memories you shared. It will make it easier for you to acknowledge that your loved one has gone on ahead. Find ways to keep the memory of your love alive; this will give you the strength to get back into your stride. You will find your space again and realise he has never really left it.

Let life happen and go with the flow. Do what you love doing. Surround yourself with people who will help you engage with life once again. It will be slow and painful but be gentle with grief. Take great care to not isolate yourself. The trouble with isolation is that you will become smaller and smaller and finally disappear.

The thing with depression that is caused by grief and loneliness is, no one can get you out of it, except you. Only you can bring yourself out of your depression, no matter how black the present is. Drag out the misery, and it controls you. There's nothing you can do about it because life continues and Life can often be a deranged bitch with a really twisted sense of humour.

Life does not permit reality to remain unchanging. Just when you think you have it all figured out with several security blankets in place, life whacks you over the head with a new experience—a new job, a new set of friends. A new love could crawl under your security blankets and kick them away. There is no proof of an afterlife with angels strumming harps or devils barbecuing sinners but we do know that this is the life we have and it isn't rocket science to figure out how to make the best of it and find your bliss again.

Sometimes you have to do the dumping

When we need to end a relationship that is going nowhere, we find ourselves making all sorts of excuses to keep it going. Our Bullshit Radar will tell us that we are in love with the idea of the relationship and not with the partner. We think if we break it off, we will not find another.

We decide better the bird in hand and we try hard to please the birdbrain, hoping we can improve him. Sometimes we decide it's easier to change ourselves and pretend to be what he wants. But, sweet thing, his DNA cannot change; neither can he. Neither can you. No one changes because one's character does not change. Some will change for a short time but they will revert to what they were. If we hope to change the other and continue in a relationship that is going nowhere, we end up resentful and depressed.

You have to do the dumping if you find yourself in an abusive or violent relationship. You have to dump and not look back if your life depended on it because if you are walking out of an abusive relationship, your life could actually depend on it.

There are too many women who fall under the spell of a highly intelligent predator. What do you do when Mister Perfect turns into Monster Perfect out to take complete control of your existence? And he does it by beating you within an inch of your life?

Learn to recognise the early signs of a monster or a bully. Prevention is better than the cure, so learn how to preempt bullying whether physical or mental, by stopping disrespect in its tracks at the outset. If you cannot stop the disrespect, then dumping is your best option.

6

Avoid Pain with this Kick-ass Compatibility Questionnaire

Have you discussed being married or have you only been focused on the wedding? Do you have questions about finances? Do you have worries about how many kids you will have? Do you discuss sex as a future married couple?

Let's see now... Like a tourist guide taking you through the life of a woman, I have led you through dating, bad relationships, putting down disrespect, dealing with mental abuse, recognising and avoiding domestic abuse, and dealing with dumping and divorce, so I cannot leave this Part 2 of the book wallowing in pain. There are ways to avoid these dangers, and the solution for much of these lies in this kick-ass questionnaire I have gone above and beyond the call of duty to think up for you.

Women have a special kind of courage. They decide they are ready for marriage and are sure they can handle it. Their parents did it and it looks like a cakewalk. They see the porcupine of marriage full of attitude with its quills upright and they laugh the light laugh. The woman coos and heads for the sweet cuddly porcupine. Six months down the line, she's pulling out the barbs crossly and saying, WTF!

As an institution, marriage has too many triggers that can split it right down the middle. No one tells us about these triggers. Everyone either jokes or gushes. But if you have niggling worries about a marriage you are planning to embark on, what do you fear the most?

When I got married, my only worry, as with most of my peers at that time, was that my guy would cheat on me. He never did (at least he didn't get caught) but we were crumbling as a unit under the weight of different issues. Finances, Unacceptable Conduct, Kids (easy enough acronym to remember) are the real perils that jigger up a marriage. But let's get the cheating out of the way first.

Dealing with cheating is simple. You have clear choices when you know your partner is cheating on you. You can leave or you can stay. If you are married and you leave through divorce, you will take your half-share of the combined assets. Assets give you stability if they are sizable, but they don't give you closure because betrayal cannot be quantified in money terms. Neither can your personal investment of giving yourself to him, your time, your energy be measured. What did you get in return? Pain and betrayal? How do you put a hard currency figure to that?

If you stay, you can turn a blind eye and live in denial, or make him regret the day he strayed. But because I'm old, wise and I know my shit, I believe if anyone cheats once, they will do it again.

You have zeroed in on The One. Joy of joys, he has chosen you too. This surely is a union made in Heaven but don't go picking out engagement rings as yet. Don't go hunting for apartments or picking out names for your children, or your cat or your dog. It is time for The Compatibility Questionnaire.

You may both be interested in a live-in relationship, or you both may be interested in marriage. Either way, if it is a long-term commitment you are after, this questionnaire will help.

If I had this when I decided to marry, I would have known that 'Things Will Sort Themselves Out' is not at all a good plan. It's a pity I was not born old and wise. I knew shit then. Now I *know* shit. That's a big difference.

If you have made your choice, be aware that both of you have certain priorities, certain fears, certain needs. Don't ignore them or hope that they will sort themselves out. They do not.

It is the little things that stress a relationship, little things that underline shared work and shared responsibilities. They are little things you never think of discussing, but the thing is, they grow into big things and then bite you in the ass.

Sit down with your significant other and ask the questions listed here. It's best for both of you to write your answers down, and then compare and discuss them. Unlike wedding vows, which are abstract and romantic and meant to add the 'awww' element to the ceremony, this compatibility questionnaire must be asked, answered and discussed, before you decide on your wedding venue.

I may be bragging here but my Compatibility Questionnaire provides the nuts and bolts of a strong domestic partnership. The points listed below pretty much cover everything in your life as a couple and a family.

You can add more that are peculiar to your situation—like if you belong to different religions, or have specific hereditary health issues. Go through them because sorting out these seemingly minor issues will give you the blueprint for your years ahead together.

A woman in her eighties recently pointed out that most men want to replace their mothers with a young, stronger wife, while women want to replace their fathers with a young, stronger husband.

The average woman wants to keep her job but needs hired help to cook and clean and wash and scrub. She wants the routine of grocery shopping to be shared. She wants electronic gadgets and a beautiful house. She needs her husband to help with the chores and housework if hired help is not affordable or absent. She wants her husband to listen, offer sympathy if required and celebrate her triumphs of the day. She wants to chat, eat, chat some more while watching television, go to bed, have a lot of foreplay, have sex, then cuddle and talk.

The average man wants someone to keep his house and his clothes clean and tidy. He wants her to greet him at the end of the day, fresh and smiling with a great meal and a sympathetic or admiring ear. He wants to watch television programmes of his choice, check his phone, have great sex, turn to the wall and sleep.

They have never discussed their priorities with each other in so many words. If they had, they might have had a rocking marriage, instead of one heading for the rocks.

Couples don't give much thought to the domestic routine that will take over their life together, running a household and raising a family. Again, there are exceptions to this rule, but most couples, friends, family and people who had written in to my agony-aunt column have battled over these three issues—conduct of the couple, how money has to be spent and how the kids have to be raised. This questionnaire therefore deals with the three biggies: Finances, Unacceptable Conduct and Kids. (Again, you are welcome to such an easy acronym.)

Finances: Single income, double income and who decides on spending and saving

The major reason for trouble in marriages is not cheating. Money, how it is to be spent and saved, causes the clashes and resentment. The solution is a personal slush fund.

You will need to have joint bank accounts: a couple of joint accounts, one with his name first, one with your name first. One will be used for spending and the other for investing your savings and surplus revenue. These accounts would be set up for covering joint and big-ticket expenses like vacations, a new house, hospitalisation, higher education and so on.

Separate from those, each of you should have a single name account where you put in a percentage of your earnings, or your combined earnings, for no-questions-asked spending. But that comes after you have begun your married life together.

Before that, the first thing you do before you book your wedding venue is to have somewhere to live. That is your first financial headache. Here is a compilation of some potentially dangerous financial flashpoints:

1. Where would you both like to live?
2. Are you both urban apartment people or house-in-the-suburbs or countryside people?
3. Would you like to travel instead of settling in your hometown?
4. Do you both prefer the freedom of renting an apartment or the solid security of owning one and putting down roots?
5. Would you continue working after marriage and enjoy financial independence?
6. Or would either of you be happy playing housewife or house-husband?
7. Would he be comfortable being a stay-at-home dad if you are pulling in serious money?
8. Will you maintain meticulous records of every expense big and small? Or will you keep a fixed amount for monthly expenses and not bother about maintaining records?
9. What about investments? Will just one person handle savings and investments? Or will you both be involved?
10. When purchases both big and small have to be made, will you consult each other on every purchase, or just go ahead and buy?
11. What about keeping money aside for fun?
12. What are your thoughts on medical insurance, loans and mortgages?
13. When do you set up investments for your children?

14. Do you both agree to start a solid pension plan for each of you immediately?
15. Or will you just meet the challenges of old age as and when they come?
16. Will both sit together while filing returns, without screaming bloody murder?
17. While lending or gifting money to others, will both discuss the issue properly before parting with joint income?

Unacceptable Conduct: Communication and cohabitation questions

1. Will both share equally in all housework-related jobs without any drama?
2. Would it be better to get paid help?
3. Who buys the groceries if both have jobs and long commutes?
4. What about going out with friends? Are you comfortable with each other's friends?
5. How much time should be spent with the in-laws? Remember, once the kids come along, it's all hands to the pump, so keep your in-laws sweet.
6. Entertaining at home, yes or no? If yes, how often? If no, are both on board with that?
7. What is the policy on bringing in surprise guests to share a meal or your roof?
8. Ground rules for arguments are vital. Should you have a rule to never let the sun go down on your anger? Do you sit down and discuss the problem? Put the minutes of the argument in an Argument Register and enter the resolution

too? What about if the argument gets heated? Raised voices allowed? Is swearing at each other allowed?

9. Do you both agree that there will be no fighting or name calling in front of the kids?
10. Do you share the same tastes in television programs? Remote control battles cause unbelievable built-up resentment if you have only one television set. Are you okay if one of you hogs the TV and the other watches online entertainment?
11. Do you have the television on during meals? What about phones and tablets? Are you both okay with focusing on online entertainment rather than focusing on each other? What happens when you have a family?
12. What about sex? Is one of you interested in trying out all positions in the Kama Sutra three times a day while the other is not?
13. Is an open marriage allowed?
14. Is either partner having doubts about their sexuality?

If you have any other questions or doubts about unacceptable conduct, discuss them now.

Kids: Questions on raising your children so society doesn't curse you

It's the raising of children that causes a lot of grief for both husband and wife. Here are some questions you might want to ask:

1. How soon after marriage does he want children?
2. How soon after marriage do you want children?

3. How many children do you both agree on? None? One? Two? Or a football team?
4. Will he be a hands-on dad? Will you both look after cleaning, feeding, burping, washing, walking and carrying the baby? Talking to it?
5. Will both be present for paediatrician visits?
6. What kind of parenting will you be following? Disciplinary, lenient, loving but firm? Or take it as it comes?
7. Will you have each other's backs when the kids play you against each other?
8. What kind of schools are you thinking of? What kind of education? Home schooling, public, private, international baccalaureate?
9. If you have a boy, what plans do you *both* have for him?
10. If you have a girl, will both of you have different plans for her?
11. How will you bring up your kids? To be independent? To help around the house? To be fine upright citizens? To be compassionate? To be courteous to all? To not back down from a fight? To finish what they begin? Or will you just let Life be their guide?
12. Will you teach your children that girls should be able to do the work that boys do and vice versa?
13. Will you teach your boys *and* your girls to sew, to paint walls as well as watercolours, to fix fuses, to do carpentry and plumbing, to pick out fabric and colours for décor, to cook, garden, to do the dishes, clean and tidy?
14. Will you stop all misogyny in your sons, no matter how young or how old they are?

15. Will you promise your children that you will not hound them to be something they are not? And if they tell you that they are not ready, unsure, afraid or incapable of a goal you wish them to achieve, you will get off their backs?

You may think these are non-issues that can be handled as your marriage progresses. I would urge you, if you are planning on taking this major step, discuss this questionnaire with your partner. It is these supposedly minor non-issues that escalate into major showdowns and wreck marriages. I don't have to tell you that they destroy children too. The answers to these questions will be the blueprint of your marriage.

It may not work out as either of you intended. He may decide this is not at all what he was expecting. He wanted sex on tap and someone to cook, clean and hostess for him and present him with children so his amazing line continues and here you are expecting that he be responsible.

You may not want to be the happy housewife; you may want to be the stressed-out corporate career woman. He could break it off, but before you fling things at me, you might consider that it is better to be dumped before marriage than to be chasing after him for alimony and child support for the rest of your life.

Part III

Notice How Family Begins With an F?

1

Pregnancy Reality Check

Do you feel that nesting-mother instinct? Do you want to hold one of your own when you see little gurgling babies? Do you have family and friends urging you to have kids? Are you planning to get pregnant?

The last time I checked, there were 7.6 billion people on this planet. I ask you why, why add any more to our giant numbers? There are more pink slips than jobs floating around. There is more concrete and asphalt than there is food and water. Big Business is making enough money; there is no imperative for you to bring one more consumer into the world. That's the broad picture. Now let's take the narrow view.

You have sex and you get knocked up with a fidgety foetus growing in your uterus. Congratulations, they cry out, so full of delight. That's cause for joy they say, but look behind the fake congratulations. There is pity there, because they know.

The women have specific knowledge that this is the end of life as you know it, for the simple reason that from here on, you will have no life of your own anymore. Partying is over. Long quiet walks are over. Pooping in peace is over. A good long bath is history. You have to think, instead, of the life growing inside of you, with hair and teeth and a rapid heartbeat. A baby changes the balance of life in the home. Yes, one baby or more can complete a home, but they can wreck life in your house as you know it.

Why would any woman in her right mind want to get pregnant? Unless, she doesn't quite know what's in store for her. So let me step in and tell you what pregnancy is all about. It's not great. In fact, it is the exact opposite of anything great.

You don't feel good, your body goes to hell and beyond, and your fabulous I-own-my-space stride turns into a waddle. Your massive belly will enter a room before you do and you will look and feel terrible. All your body parts begin acting weird. Your nose and ankles will compete with each other to get fat and swollen.

You feel tired all the time. You can never get comfortable, while sitting, lying down, or standing, and you feel like peeing every fifteen minutes. You feel hungry and nauseous at the same time. The stuff you used to love eating makes you physically ill, and you have weird cravings for the strangest foods. Morning sickness lasts the whole freaking day and it hits you at unexpected times. Sometimes someone's body odour in an enclosed space can make you heave.

In all your examinations in your first trimester, you have to go to the gynaecologist, which is an experience nothing short of hellish. They tell you to relax. What a joke. Unless it's changed now, this was my experience. My business-end was completely naked on the examining table, my feet thrust through stirrups and my thighs spread wide open. And they tell you to relax? The doctor slides an ice-cold metal speculum up your vagina, and then the gloved finger moves all over checking the uterus and the cervix. The experience is extremely uncomfortable and humiliating. I hear it's changed in some clinics where they just press parts of your belly and keep the speculum for the 37th week, but until four years ago, women went through the speculum.

Other women get scary

Baby bumps of pregnant women become a magnet for all women who have already had kids. My ob-gyn Dr Marie told me, 'Get it out of your head that they mean well. If you can get away, do it, but they will corner you to tell you stories that will scare the shit out of you.' No one knows why they do this.

There was this monster who attached herself to me and told me how one of her babies had a head the size of a melon and how her vagina tore before the doctor could make a proper cut and how till today she has no control over 'going to the toilet'. I asked her which end, but she walked away in horror. I never got to know which sphincter of hers was non-operational.

Random people will ask you all sorts of questions. They will ask you who your ob-gyn is. Then they tell you to leave your obstetrician because he or she is no good. They will tell you of his or her botched deliveries. They will tell you to transfer to their obstetrician. They will insist you write down his or her particulars.

Others stare at your belly and predict with conviction whether it will be a boy or a girl. I hope it's a puppy, a pony would be nice too, I told quite a few. Then they'd back away from me and I could return in peace to my book.

Women out to scare you are like wild animals. It is important that you do not make eye contact with them. Do not encourage conversation because they *will* savage you.

The trimesters

You begin thinking in weeks and trimesters. From the time you pee on a stick and it tells you that you are pregnant, to the time you push your placenta out, it's weeks, not months, that you think about.

The first trimester is the first three months. This thing is supposed to last for three trimesters, so, nine months, right? Wrong. Full term is supposed to be forty weeks. But forty weeks is almost ten months, isn't it? No, they say, pregnancy term is counted according to lunar months, which are calculated at twenty-nine-and-a-half days. The first trimester is from one to twelve weeks. The second is from thirteen to twenty-eight weeks and the third is from twenty-nine to forty weeks.

Polycystic Ovary Disease (PCOD) sends hormones out of whack, which results in very irregular and very painful periods, acne, weight gain, insulin resistance, hair on your head thinning and falling but, oh, thick hair growing furiously in places where it really should not. You get hair on your face, on your chin, on your chest, on your arms, on your legs and on your upper back. And it becomes almost impossible to conceive.

You tend to think that's a good thing, but then out of the blue you find that the irregular menstrual period you had gotten used to is actually pregnancy. The PCOD should not matter now, but it does and you have to take hormonal treatment for months in the most awful manner possible. You take the treatments by injection and by vaginal and rectal suppositories. The miracle of birth, they call it. What a joke.

As the pregnancy progresses, the baby gets larger. Your ankles swell, you cannot sleep, the baby keeps moving and kicking around. If you think you are sleep-deprived when you are pregnant, imagine what is going to happen when that baby is born and starts fretting just when you lie down. Notice, I have not spoken about the actual delivery. Oh no, that experience deserves an entire chapter of its own.

Meanwhile, your belly grows bigger and even bigger. Your back aches and now you want to pee every fifteen minutes. Your breasts look like melons and you cringe when you look at yourself in a mirror. Your face looks swollen and your body warped beyond recognition. Yes, maybe not you, but it happens too often to too many pregnant women to not warn you.

You cease to look on the father of the foetus as the love of your life and you find it easy to transfer that love and commitment to the child.

The cheating husband

Then there's this other phenomenon of the cheating husband. Yes, yes, not your husband, other husbands, but you should keep it in mind. In that halcyon period before you got pregnant, sex was all he could think of when you were around. He just had to know you were awake to be all over you like a rash. Sex three times a day was a regular thing. You loved it too. But then pregnancy is the great speed bump in those early years of sex on tap.

You just don't feel up to it when you are pregnant. By the time the morning sickness ends, you are about the size of an old whale. And the man still wants sex. You are totally unattractive but he still wants sex. You can't bend down to fasten your shoes, but he still wants sex. It's not always the man though. Often pregnant women get amazingly horny. And you make love like a couple of porcupines—very carefully.

Observe the men congratulating you on your pregnancy. There is pity in their eyes when they look at your husband. They know that regular sex is over for him. Wining and dining will now be replaced by whining while dining. It is at this time that husbands look for sexual gratification elsewhere. Yes, yes, not your husband, other husbands. Ditto after the baby is born. Which is why, if your guy is not going to be a hands-on dad, you could have a different set of problems on your hands.

He won't get any time to even glance at other women if he is involved in planning for the baby, getting the equipment ready—sterilizer, diapers, diaper-disposal service, a better washing machine, feeding bottles, nipples, brushes, a bassinet maybe, or a cot. Acidity and indigestion are part of the pregnancy deal, so it's a good idea to get him to rub your belly gently so you can fart. Learn to fart in his presence. It's very empowering.

After the baby is born, he has to be a hands-on dad doing everything you do including feeding the baby with formula or breast milk pumped and stored in the refrigerator. If both of you are exhausted together, yours is the only bed the guy will be crawling into.

Should you opt for a Caesarean section or normal vaginal delivery?

People tell you to go in for a C-section; others vote for the vaginal delivery for getting back on your feet faster. Let me tell you, both suck. You will not have the trauma of forcing a three-kilo ham out of your vagina with a C-section, nor will the baby go through its own trauma of being squeezed out of a narrow opening for hours on end. If you don't start hobbling around a few hours after you come out of anaesthesia, it will take you a month before you can walk properly after a C-section.

With a natural delivery, if the baby's head is large, they cut your vaginal wall so that it does not tear. After the baby and the afterbirth emerge from your body, the cut is stitched and those stitches hurt like bitches when they tighten. But it's not as incredibly horrendous as the pain of labour. That pain is just obscene. There is no other word to describe it.

I had two natural deliveries. Why two? Because I believed the sadistic old liars in my family who assured me the second delivery is easy. It was not. The second time round, my kid had been doing gymnastics in the womb and the umbilical cord had twisted three times around her neck. I heard my obstetrician groan, 'Oh shit!' I hated the torture of labour and delivery so much that I showed up the mandatory two years after the second delivery and demanded a tubectomy.

My advice is, if you have your husband and one other family member or paid help to cook, clean and wash, then a C-section is just the ticket. You swan around in bed doing mild exercises and let everyone pamper you until you can walk with ease. Talk to your doctor and get all the information you can.

Doctors hate it when you have specific knowledge or even vague knowledge and start questioning them or telling them about your 'research'. So the best thing to do is read up on pregnancy and delivery, keep a small notebook and, as the question comes to your mind, write it down in the book and read it out to the doctor at your next visit.

What I'm putting forward here, and you may or may not think it is a good idea, is that we have enough humans on this planet. There is absolutely no need to add to our numbers. Enjoy your life, use protection, spend your money on things that you love to do, help others, but don't go through all that torture just because society dictates that you need to have children, preferably boys.

This is just the pregnancy. Now let's deal with the delivery.

2

The Horror of the Vaginal Delivery

Did you think labour was just a bit of pain, some sweat and straining? Do you think natural delivery is better than a C-Section? Do you think an epidural always works? Did you know the placenta has to be squeezed out too?

Forty weeks pass. It's D-Day or Delivery Day, or Labour Day or God-Just-Let-Me-Die-Now Day. You are awash with mega cramps that you cannot get your hands on to massage away. The cramping is happening deep inside your womb. You feel a small explosion in your pants. You check. No one mentioned the bloody mucus that makes an appearance. Aghast, I hollered details to my mom downstairs, and all excited she said, 'That's the "red show"! Your baby is on the move.' Later I learned it is the mucus plug at the mouth of the cervix that is expelled first. I won't pretend—it's a disgusting sight. The sight of it together with the cramping makes you want to gag.

It is at precisely this point that it dawns on you how completely that early session of 'lovemaking' has fucked you up. Your lover went through your body from the outside in and knocked happily on your cervix; the foetus is going to do the same in the opposite direction.

Your cervix will widen slowly, ever so slowly, taking even up to twenty hours, to accommodate that big head. Your baby will tear through the sac holding the amniotic fluid. The amniotic fluid gushes out. They say, 'Your water has broken'. And everyone gets all excited, ooh, ooh, the baby is on the way. You know that baby is on the way because the contractions get worse. They give you an enema so that you do not pass a stool when the baby is being born. An enema!

The mother of all pain

Forget what the pregnancy books tell you. They talk of contractions. Contractions. Such an inadequate word for the agony that follows. The pain is nothing you can ever be prepared for. It is the Mother of all Pain, it is the fine print in a contract; it is a combination of aches, cramps, stabs, spasms and finally, a sea of continuous, all-pervasive, unbelievable wrenching, tearing agony. You are screaming that you want to die, begging them to let you die. And surprise surprise, in many cases, the epidural does not work.

The things they do!

You feel a sharp biting pain on the rim of your vagina. It's the doctor cutting into the wall so the vagina does not tear. Irony much? This is serious stuff, but all that bastard doctor does is call out to you to push, push and push again. And you summon up all the rage and strength and despair in you to give that last final squeezing of all the muscles you can think of and it's done. Good, good, good, the doctors say, well done.

The afterbirth

The baby comes out pretty revolting to look at, covered in bloody streaks and liquid, and you think the torture is over when you hear your baby cry. But no, oh no, it's not over for you. It's never over for you, you poor slob. There's the afterbirth still to be sorted out.

The afterbirth is the placenta and the amniotic sac that have to come out now, and you have to push again to get it out of your poor tortured body. They never show expulsion of the placenta in the movies, not even in horror movies. Then they stitch you up and leave you to think about the sucky life decisions you have made while they sort out your baby.

The radiating agony of labour made your jaws and the back of your neck feel like some giant monster tied them in knots. Now your nerves begin to relax. Sometimes you get the rigours. Your body shakes like a leaf, and even after you have been stitched up and dumped on a recovery bed, the rigours continue. My daughter took forty-five minutes to stop shaking after delivering my grandchild. I wanted to kill people and smash things. But I was soothing her and smiling gently and telling her what a trooper she was. I felt it was not the right time to remind her that ever since their third birthdays, I had been instructing both my daughters not to marry and if they did marry, not to have children. Did they listen? No.

Meeting your baby and falling in love

They bring your rinsed infant and put her in your arms. And you feel a welling up of love of biblical proportions. How can you not? That baby looks so innocent, so vulnerable. She's yours, flesh of your flesh, bone of your bone. You feel it because that is what they told you you would feel. The same story has come down over the centuries. If you have given birth to a child, there is an invisible bond that will never be broken. See? Again something that is invisible and we blindly accept that too.

My theory about that pulsing, glowing love is that you feel such a wave of relief and accomplishment that you single-handedly pushed a living creature as large as a good-sized ham out of your vagina and without using your own hands at that. How can you not marvel at your achievement? That massive head coming out of that tiny vagina is the only miracle of birth that I am willing to acknowledge.

More to the point, the obscene pain has stopped. Now you just feel sore. Sore is fine. Sore makes you wince, not scream out bloodcurdling pleas to let you die. The relief is huge and overwhelming. Your hormones are all over the place. It's an easy progression of thought to package that overriding relief from pain as maternal love.

The hospital lulls you into a false sense of security. Through your short stay at the hospital, they wash and tend to your baby, handle the medication, its drops, etcetera, and only bring it to you washed and talc-ed for you to place at your breast.

Recovery

Those breasts that you were once so proud of are engorged with milk, swollen and hard, leaking and bloody painful. Sometimes the baby refuses to latch on to your nipples and you think, oh god, I'm a bad mother. They call in a harried nurse who gives you techniques to feed that infant. Finally, if all else fails, the breast pump they made you pack in your hospital bag is brought in and takes centrestage in your life.

Your vagina is healing. It had stretched so much and was cut and stitched. As the days go by, the stitches dry and tighten ruthlessly and you cannot sit or walk properly. Now they have soluble stitches; mine had to be removed on Day Six. I try to kill that memory. I still see new mothers sitting gingerly on one butt cheek just the way I did, so I guess technology notwithstanding, the pain is the same.

Added to that, you have to take care that infection does not set in, so you have to wash your traumatized vagina that has just seen more action than it cares to remember with a very hot antimicrobial solution. This is done every time you use the toilet. The sensation is horrible.

If you are constipated, they give you a laxative because it

is verboten to strain during a bowel movement because all hell would break loose if your stitches were to open.

Sometimes the laxative does not work because with all the strain of childbirth, you find you have also developed a nice rosette of painful swollen piles around your anus, so an enema is administered. It is a perfectly horrible exercise. And they call it the joy of motherhood. Bastards.

Childbirth has to be the most vicious trick pulled on women

The Bible is pretty bald about it. It explains childbirth as the curse of God on womankind because disobedient Eve ate of the fruit of the Tree of Knowledge and gave some to her partner Adam. This was done despite instructions to the contrary by God himself. So being the Alpha Male, God got mad at them for having the power of accessing and using as much knowledge as He did. Then He got all insecure about how they could also eat of the fruit of the Tree of Life and live as long as He, so He booted them out of the Garden of Eden, before they discovered that tree too.

And as if that were not bad enough, He cursed Womankind forevermore to bring out their children in pain. Insecure or what? Don't believe me? Read *Genesis*. That's what God told the angel when asked why he got so mad at the First Couple.

A Caesarean section is a piece of cake compared to natural delivery

More and more women are thinking that nothing and no one is worth the agony of labour and natural childbirth, so they opt for a Caesarean section. Here the pain is postpartum. It's a major operation and you have to be careful not to lift heavy weights, which is ridiculous when you think about it. You have just had a heavy baby taken out of your middle and that baby will get heavier by the day. Before opting for a C-section, make sure you have someone to shop, cook and clean for you and the baby for at least three months. Your job is to feed your baby and love her or him.

I have seen recovery processes in both forms of delivery in the recent past and the C-section, when compared with a natural delivery, is a piece of cake. The only painful part is swollen ankles and those can be fixed with walking a little, but often, six or eight hours after the surgery. That's painful, yes, but you don't scream with the pain. You wince. The few steps you take every hour or so gets your blood circulation up and about, helping you heal quicker. Even up and down alongside your bed while holding your drip is fine. But you must walk. It is painful, but the pain is a mere tickle compared with what awaits you in a natural delivery when the epidural does not work.

Get those tubes tied

Grown men turn pale when asked to get a vasectomy. It's a thirty-minute procedure for men, but they prefer the woman gets sterilized. It's a half-day procedure for a woman. The tubectomy or laparoscopy itself takes about thirty minutes, but you are put under total anaesthesia. Two tiny incisions are made in your abdomen and your fallopian tubes are tied. Waiting for the anaesthesia to wear off takes a good half day, and you are sore for anything between one and three weeks. I was sore for two days, because I was so happy I got my tubes tied. After that you are free from one major pregnancy worry. Also, if you do feel like straying, you won't be bringing outside genes into the family tree. But the bottom line is, we have enough humans on this planet.

3

Babies Take Over Your Life

Babies are not sweet-smelling.
Babies are not sweet-tempered.
Sleep deprived? Cracked nipples? Babies don't give a damn.

Now you are a brand-new mother. You realise life did a number on you when you find yourself standing in your own house with your newborn in your arms. The awful reality closes in on you that you are now responsible for raising this human being. You look around and you don't see hospital staff to clean and wash and iron, no hospital cooks to provide you with healthy milk-producing viands, no doctors and nurses to check the baby's vitals and provide medication.

This little human, just a few days old, will depend on you for all its needs—food, clothing, bathing, cleaning, combing, brushing, washing, powdering, medicating, counselling and unconditional loving. You will have to launder clothes and diapers. There will be pee diapers that will make your eyes water and your lungs spasm if you leave them lying around. You will gag over poop diapers. The smell never quite leaves the room. Or your hair. Or your hands.

You will have to measure formula and tonics and vitamins. You will have to maintain meticulous records of doctors' visits and shots received and a schedule of shots to be received. You will have to factor in breast-feeding too. You will be asked to choose between manual breast pumps and electric ones. Potty training will turn you potty. That is a given.

And then there's that whole psychology thing. You have to bring up the child in a wholesome, caring, encouraging environment or else you will unleash a monster on society and be forever damned. Discipline is important, but how do you not turn into Attila the Hun on that poor child?

You learn quickly enough that having the baby around does not exempt you from doing your regular household duties. The cooking and cleaning, dusting, mopping, they're all there waiting for you. The shopping, paying the bills, going to the bank, collecting the post, taking out the garbage, feeding the dog, doing the correspondence, entertaining visitors.

Oh yes, the visitors. There will be a stream of them tramping through the house. Why? They turn up like the Magi because new babies are a human magnet. Random neighbours, friends and relatives walk in the front door clutching some gaily wrapped gift like it is their passport into your home, their faces stretched into inane smiles of delight. Watch how they lean forward as though expecting to see the Sultan of Brunei's jewels. They pick up the baby you just put to sleep after a bloody long time and rock it and cuddle it.

Of course, the baby, still unused to undiluted sounds and smells, objects to the new hands and smell of strange adults. Its nose wrinkles and its entire face crumples in a horrible dark red mix of rage and discomfort. The soft little body feels as hard as a giant piece of ginger as the visitor quickly hands your squalling red monster back to you.

You want to hit the visitor really hard but you cannot. You smile sweetly and coo at the baby while the visitors crowd around and loudly try to decide who the kid looks like. You are too tired to tell them that your baby looks exactly like the courier guy.

Life gets too much to handle. This is the time mothers generally get the blues. Postpartum depression, they call it. There have been incidents when mothers have turned into murderers during this time of psychological shutdown. Which is why before that should happen, get help. Not necessarily a shrink. It may not be psychiatric help that you require.

You need people around you who will not let you feel overwhelmed. You need someone to help you with your chores. You need someone to ease the burden of being a new mother. You need people around who understand that you are going through postpartum depression.

Most mothers feel overwhelmed, irritable, exhausted and a lack of confidence in their ability to get through the day, so don't feel bad about yourself—it's normal. According to the experts I've read, around 15 percent of mothers feel clinically depressed. If you feel like hurting yourself or others, seek professional help and be open about what you feel. You can get out of it. It is a serious illness but it is completely treatable.

You have emerged from the most traumatic experience it is a woman's misfortune to experience. But do the rest of your family or neighbours even care? They say pooh, motherhood is a blessing; the whole world has been born and mothers have been doing this all their lives, enough with the drama already...

You have to put your foot down and put it down hard. Insist on paid or unpaid help. Your job is to love that kid, so love that kid. Let the others do the work, until you feel strong enough to do it yourself. Even then, if you don't feel like doing domestic chores, hire help if you can swing it. Do not attempt to be Superwoman because the simple truth is, no one cares.

You may tell yourself that it is quicker doing the chores yourself, but remember, the rest of the family is quite happy with you doing all the work. They're human beings; human beings are selfish. That baby of yours is going to grow up into them. So delegate chores.

If you get help at this time, of course you will accept it gratefully, but if it is a mother or a mother-in-law, you will be reminded of it for the rest of your life. Thank them for pitching in and show gratitude, but if they get offensive, tell them you will help change their diapers too in a few years.

If your husband changes the baby's diaper just once or twice, he will expect a national medal of honour. Yes, yes, there are a growing number of saintly husbands who help without being asked. But there are too many of the other kind too. Be prepared to find that yours may be one such. Now do you see how important that Compatibility Questionnaire is?

You will think that all this is worth it when the baby looks into your eyes and smiles like an angel. Don't be fooled. If your baby is just a few weeks old, it could be that he or she is passing gas. A good fart gives the baby pleasure. The smile after six weeks is a 'social smile'. The baby considers you a good fart. That baby can scream like a banshee when hungry or wet or not burped properly.

You set your baby down in the brand-new baby cot you bought because it had such a story-book look to it. Point to note: If you have the space and the money, buy a cot, but it is a waste of space and money. Put that baby in a bed and invest in a safety railing around it. I digress, however... back to the baby cot. You place your newborn in it and your baby begins fussing at this alien environment. It wants to be held in your warm embrace. So you pick it up again and croon softly. It stops fussing and you think, wow, I'm a mother! I have the power to make this child of mine happy. I will be a great mother.

You will be so wrong because the baby thinks so *that's* it. If I fuss and scream, this milk lady will obey my every wish.

Babies are not angels. They know nothing of kindness or compassion. Babies are self-taught in the art of manipulation from the get-go. They know if they cry long and loud you will be at their side ready to go through fire and ice to cater to their every whim. They also know you will do anything, ANYTHING, they demand, for blessed silence. They learn that early because babies are great observers of the human condition.

You have lost the battle before it can begin. You cannot be tough with the baby because come on, it is one-eighteenth of your size and you are no monster.

You need to be cunning, to anticipate trouble and forestall it. That is just to make sure that the baby grows into a balanced, well-adjusted human being who will not be a burden on society. Yeah, this whole thing is not just confined to you and your baby and maybe your family members. Society too is a stakeholder in how you bring up your child.

There's scheduling, chores and sleep. They say sleep when the baby sleeps, but then when do you do the chores? So you give up on sleep sometimes and on chores at other times.

Your back aches, you smell nasty with a combination of sweat, baby burp and baby poop. You begin to see double because you have not had a really good sleep in months. You have not really had a proper bath. You have to eat and drink properly so that you can breastfeed your baby for at least six months, to build up its immunity as well as its character. At least this is what the experts say, though I cannot see how sucking your mother's nipple raw will give you a good character later on in life.

They say breast-fed babies grow into well-adjusted, healthy, intelligent people. I'm betting that is another black lie thought up to keep the mother bound to the cradle. I have known formula-fed babies who are as sweet or as irritating as breastfed babies. I have known breast-fed babies who are as susceptible to illnesses as are formula-fed babies. It means that as long as the baby is breastfed, you cannot go out for a night on the town. If you do, you will have to take the baby along and when it is feeding time, you have to suffer the public indignity of your breasts leaking and spreading milk stains on your clothes.

They tell you that caring for a baby gets easier as the child grows. Sorry, sweetheart, as the baby grows, so do your problems. Expenses mount, trips to doctors increase. Rows of medicine and vitamin bottles are lined up like an invading army on your dresser. The good thing is it doesn't last forever, only for the next eighteen or twenty years.

You have visitors coming in with Advice and Tips and Shortcuts. What to use for teething, what to avoid, how to keep the baby's fever down, the fear of convulsions. They will tell you horror stories of crib deaths that will destroy any last bits of sleep you can snatch. Now you are afraid to leave the baby alone, terrified of crib death.

If you can snatch fifteen minutes or half an hour, make some time for yourself. It is mother's love, they say, but experience has taught me this: if your every thought is about the baby, if every plan you make is for the baby, if every action you make is for the baby, then you are setting yourself up for a bad fall, my friend. First, you ignore your husband, completely forgetting that he's the one you will finally end your days with. Ignoring him would be a huge mistake. Involve him in baby management.

If you look at it practically, he is the one responsible for creating this little human who has you on the run 24×7. It's only logical that he share the work, the planning and execution of Project Young Individual. Secondly, that baby will grow up and leave you when higher studies, work and marriage happen. So be smart. See the bigger picture and step back a little.

Remember, babies are always watching you. Make sure you are two steps ahead at all times. They look for insecurities and find them. They can smell fear and panic. Get a grip on yourself so you can get through early parenthood with some grace.

4

It's Not That Difficult to Be a Good Mother

Your boys must understand that not only are girls equal, they are definitely not the weaker sex. Your girls must know that you have their back at all times. Teach your girls and boys about good touch and bad touch. Never relax your vigilance.

Major preaching alert, but I feel so strongly about this that it hurts. If you want to go in for parenting, make your parenthood count. It is not only your peers who will judge you. It is not only society that will judge you. Your children will judge you once they reach adolescence and develop a sense of persecution. Some don't outgrow adolescence when it comes to blaming their parents. And their judgement can really hurt. It's not easy being a good mother, but it's not that difficult either, once you get the hang of it.

You cannot change the world. You cannot change genetic patterns, but what you can do every step of the way is to let your children know that you have their back and that you love them fiercely. Not desperately. Fiercely. Which means you can thump them when they step out of line. Do your kids know you have their back at all times?

Sometimes it's difficult when a child treats you like unpaid help or asks too much of you, but you are the reason they are here, so you have to swallow your spleen and step up to help out.

How do you do this? By talking to your children when they are in the womb, and continuing to talk and to listen to them and engage with them honestly whenever possible because every so often, good parents have to lie. When your children can talk to you openly and without anxiety, that's most parental problems over and done with.

You do know that women can do almost any job that men can do? In the past I used to say except be king or emperor or pee standing. Now we have democracy and there's a 'pee-buddy' contraption that women can use to pee standing. All it takes for your child to take gender equality as a given is for you to treat your girls as well as you treat your boys. It's even better when your boys and girls, your neighbours and friends and office colleagues see you challenging misogyny wherever you see it.

Once you turn into a parent, the real work begins

You have found the guy who is a perfect fit for you. You have married him and you think this is it. You have your baby or babies. You are on the highway to your happily ever after. Sorry, sweetheart, shit just got real. The real work begins now.

You have created life, given birth and now you have the job of raising world citizens. Life has folded you in its tough embrace.

If your mother forced you to follow the unfair rules of society from infancy, you don't have to continue it. Give those girls of yours a chance at the thrill of life. Dreams and goals are not the sole territory of your boys. The world belongs to your girls too, and it is your job to help them claim what is theirs.

Mud washes off little girls as easily as it washes off little boys

When your girl is little, if she wants to play in the mud, let her. Mud washes off little girls as easily as it washes off little boys. If she punches her brothers or cousins when they bully her, give her your unwavering support and let her bullies, their parents and her, see your support.

If she laughs a full-throated open-mouthed laugh that convulses her entire body, laugh along with her; do not frown and shush her and tell her that ladies don't laugh loudly. Medical science says that the full-throated body-convulsing laugh is excellent for physical health. Giggling and tittering, not much.

Do you treat her like a doll and dress her up in frills and lace? Or do you let her wear what she wants? She is a little human who wants to be comfortable. Offer her clothes that she is comfortable in. Will you introduce her to cosmetics when she is barely five? Or will you let her enjoy her childhood?

When you tell her stories, let them be adventure stories of courage and fun and confidence. For every fairy tale of a princess who marries a prince and lives happily ever after, read her books of adventure too. Give that naturally inquiring mind of hers food for thought in the books you gift her. For every doll and kitchen set she receives, get her a toy car and an engineering set too.

Teach her that her body is her own

As soon as she can understand instructions, tell your daughter that her body is her own and no one is allowed to touch her inappropriately. After the age of three, teach her to wash and dry her genital area and tell her that she should not allow anyone else to touch her there. Tell her a doctor may have to examine her there, but you or a nurse will be present in the room too. Don't show any embarrassment when you tell her these things. She has to understand that her body is her own and she alone has sole right over it.

Tell her if anyone touches her inappropriately, she should tell you about it immediately, no matter who the person may be. Protect her as much as you can without making her paranoid. It is impossible to ask a child to be on her or his guard and to figure out which human beings are friendly and which are predators. You cannot tell your toddlers to not be friendly with strangers or family or friends, who grab them and carry them all the time, so it is your job to stay close and be watchful.

You have to keep an eagle eye out on strangers, family and friends' behaviour with your child, because the child predators first set out to charm the parents, generally the mothers of the victims. Once the parent's guard is down, they move in on the child. Predators are not always strangers. You can never relax your guard.

Very often, closet paedophiles are found among friends and family members. You have to be on the alert, Mom; never let your vigilance drop. Watch out for any changes in the child's behaviour, if he or she is suddenly withdrawn, or afraid. If you see any kind of bruising on her body, ask her how she got it.

Don't let your toddlers wander off away from your line of sight. If they don't like holding your hand, invest in a leash, never mind the people giving you the stink eye. They will be the first to condemn you for losing her.

Be on constant alert with regard to paedophiles, but let her run and play, skin her knees, get coated in dust and mud. Just be around your kids; predators keep away when they know the parent is alert and watchful.

Talk to her about menstruation

When she crosses the age of eight, talk to her in a matter-of-fact manner about menstruation. Tell her that menstruation happens to all girls and all female animals, that it is the body's way of cleaning itself internally. That it is absolutely nothing to worry about. Tell her it is nothing to be ashamed of, either.

There is no need to speak of menstrual periods in whispers and code words.

Tell her to order sanitary pads in a normal voice and don't for chrissakes tell her that when she is menstruating she cannot do this, that or the other. Tell her that women can do anything and everything while menstruating—the world will not end. That rule too was made by a misogynistic society.

Above all, teach her not to be afraid or in awe of men

Teach her to treat men like she should treat all living things, with courtesy and respect. But just as with all living creatures, four-legged, two-legged and creepy-crawlies, she must step away when they make her uncomfortable.

There comes that age when she starts noticing boys because the boys will have started noticing her. This is a time when you have to have your A-game running, Mom, and you have to have her back at all times. I cannot stress enough how important it is for her to know, without any doubt, that she has your support, even when she is being obnoxious.

Let her know that she can bring her boyfriends home. This is fiendishly devious because it will give you a chance to wean her away from the creepy ones. Also, when a boy has accepted your hospitality, has shared a meal with her family, he'd have to be a complete scoundrel to hurt your girl.

Teach her to defend herself from creeps. One of the best gifts you can give her is a course in self-defense and maybe a weapon, a taser, a can of pepper spray or a six-inch serrated knife. Make sure she learns how to use whatever you get her.

Do not belittle her or criticize her choice of boyfriend. Let her know you respect her decision even though you wish you could take a flexible cane to him and chase him down the street. Once she knows that there is no opposition from you, decisions become smoother for her. If she is headstrong, she may pursue a relationship with a useless character just because you oppose it.

Tell her a relationship decision is a life-changing one. It will stick with her throughout her life. Tell her there is an element of risk no matter how nice the guy is, but no matter what, you will always be looking out for her. You will do it because that is your job, Mom. And because it's your job, the smart thing to do would be to keep your bonds with your children strong.

Why it's important you keep in touch with your kids

No matter how irritating and abrasive they may be, do not allow your relationship with your children to be put at risk at any time. I don't mean that you need to be friends with them just so that when you are sick and dying, they will fly to your bedside and be tender ministering angels. Invest wisely so that you can buy the services of a tender ministering angel and not depend on your children or relatives when you are old and bedridden. Unless, of course, your children drop everything and fly to your bedside, sack your hired nurse and take up the handling of your care themselves. Okay, that happens once in a very blue moon so don't hold your breath. Invest wisely for your bed-ridden days.

You need to keep the love burning bright between you and your children because as long as you live, they are your responsibility. You are not theirs. It's easier to shoulder your responsibility when you love them.

You created them. You are responsible for them. You have to accept that you will drop everything if they need your help at any time, whether they are sixteen weeks old in your uterus and you are heading for a miscarriage and have to give up a career you excel at to save their lives, or if they are sixty-six and you are ninety-eight and they just need to vent.

Your children may be separate entities when they grow up, but they are you—a vital part of your body. If your head had a problem or your butt had a problem, you would take immediate action to solve those problems. It's the same with your children. They are flesh of your flesh and bone of your bone. Even if they are buttheads, they are a part of you. It's simple cause and effect, actually. You are responsible for bringing them into this world, therefore you are responsible for their well-being.

With your grown daughter (or your son for that matter, but this book is primarily for girls and women) you have to be the wind beneath her wings, unseen but present at all times. Someone that she is sure is always with her. She should know that you are just a phone call and a travel ticket away. She has to know that your door is always open to her, no matter how ridiculous you may think her emergency is. You will get mad at her. You will quarrel. You will have misunderstandings, but through all that, you have to let her know that you are always there for her. One hundred percent.

Tips for bringing up your son

Teach him compassion, courtesy and respect for all living things. Show zero tolerance for any signs of misogyny in him from infancy. It would be an excellent thing if you could stretch that zero tolerance for misogyny to the men around you. Nip it in the bud.

Keep an eye out for any bullying in his character. If he bullies a girl, whether it is his sister or cousin or classmate, do not give his behaviour that boys-will-be-boys shrug. Tell him in all seriousness that you will not tolerate it. Tell him he will not speak disrespectfully to any girl or woman. He must treat the girls he meets as he should treat everyone else he interacts with—with courtesy and friendliness. Let there be no negotiation on that.

Let him know that he must not treat girls any differently from the way he treats boys. Girls should not be treated as fragile creatures. Girls must be treated as equals. They are not the weaker sex. How can they be? The future of human existence depends on them.

You know that girls grow into women who will carry a 3.5 kilo living baby deep inside their bodies and then eject it in the vilest way possible. Boys and men can barely handle a pimple squeezed on their faces. Dispense with the idea that boys must treat girls as the weaker sex. Tell your sons no special treatment for girls but no special ill-treatment of girls either. Do the world a favour and teach your sons this from the moment they can understand simple instructions.

When they reach the age of three, teach your sons how to

bathe themselves and to keep all spaces where the sun doesn't shine, clean and dry. They also have to be told that they should not allow anyone to touch their penis or buttocks. Refer to his penis as a penis.

It is a body part that does not determine his importance on earth. It has two important duties though—ridding his body of toxins and helping create your grandchildren. Tell him later when he is in his teens and ogling girls that he must use it responsibly because that penis of his can create and also destroy lives.

For every car and engineering set you buy your son, buy him a kitchen set too. Give him chores to do around the house. As soon as he can understand, let him know you expect him to help without being asked. Teach him how to cook and clean, teach him about colours and design—his wife and children will thank you for that. Knowledge of these jobs will also make him a self-sufficient man. If your husband objects, teach him to cook and clean too.

You've been there and done that, you know full well that women are struggling to survive in this world. From the womb to the tomb, the woman has to slog to succeed anywhere. Foetuses are aborted in many societies just because they are female, girl babies are killed or abandoned, schoolgirls have to fight off sexual assaults and it gets worse as they grow older. Women grow up with a fear of men in most societies.

How can we watch our girls walk in fear? Will you step up and show your boys and the men in your family how it is done? Treat all boys and men the same way that you treat all girls and women. Not just in your own family but strangers too.

How I schooled a mean five-year-old boy and ruined everyone's lunch

I gave the anti-misogyny message to a five-year-old boy not so long ago. This little boy had learned that yanking his older sister's hair in an upward wrench above her ears made her shriek and weep. He also pinched her for good measure. Yank, weep, pinch… yank, weep, pinch… They were sitting at this plush restaurant and, to his bad luck, I was at the next table.

It was my special day in the year, on which I treat myself as I would my best friend. The unpleasantness of the boy bullying his sister was harshing my mellow.

Their young mother was studying the menu and absently telling her daughter not to cry so loud. She did not say a word to her son. The boy continued the attack. The little girl, who would have been seven years old, was weeping. The mother shushed her again.

I rose, stood in front of the boy, selected his fine long curly hair above each ear and yanked upwards, hard. I also pinched him. Hard. He shrieked. The other diners looked at me in horror and disgust, like they had collectively bitten into a live caterpillar.

'What is *wrong* with you?' the young mother shrieked. The little girl was terrified. I addressed the boy, asked him if it hurt him. He was yelling with abandon now, tears coursing down his face. The mother continued shrilling. I squatted down near the boy so that we were at eye level. I told him in a quiet voice that I would be watching him. Wherever he was, I would be watching him because I had magic. And if he hurt his sister again, I would know. And I would deal with him. Because I had magic. The mother stopped shrilling. She looked mortified.

I told the little girl to never let him or *anyone* bully her again, but she was crying too hard to listen. I did not speak to the mother. I returned to my table, a stately procession of one, and ate unwisely but well. The restaurant was quiet. I had effectively ruined everyone's lunch. But hey, no pain, no gain in the war for equal treatment for all.

5

Rat-Race Vs Brat-Race for Working Moms

Did you have to give up your job when you got pregnant? Are you ready to get back to work but have no help at home? Do you feel deep guilt being a working mom? Are you considering working from home?

Your baby is now walking around, not quite potty-trained, which means you are going completely potty. You had to leave your job to have this baby, but now you are fed up to the teeth. Your deep desire to have conversations other than those of feeds, poop frequency, poop colour and odour, nappy rash, teething and vomit has reached a level of Red Alert desperation. You need mental stimulation and human interaction of the workplace as opposed to the sounds and smells of the nursery. Most of all you need the extra money.

You need new clothes too because nothing you wore prior to pregnancy fits you anymore. So you sally forth to buy some. The apparel store's changing-room four-walled mirrors impassively tell you how your body shape has changed for the worse. My changing rooms showed me where it was flat, there was bulge; where there was rounded beauty, there were bags and rippling thunder thighs. I did not like that one little bit. I was never ramp-worthy, but I was fit. I learned very quickly to never ever buy body-sculpting innerwear if you are commuting and working regular hours.

So you buy body-sculpting innerwear and it is always frightfully expensive. You find out later you cannot wear it for ten straight hours of the day, sitting upright and walking around in an office *and* doing a two-hour commute, without wanting to commit mass murder. You do what you should have done the first time—you buy elegant but comfortable clothes. Then you can focus on the job.

If you took on a job without setting your systems in place both at the office and at your home, keeping the job itself becomes a tightrope. You had wanted an escape from the routine of a noisy baby and the boredom of housework, but at the end of ten hours of tedious office work and noisy commute, you have to return to the noisy baby and the tedium of household chores. That never goes away, even if you have household help.

Most working moms don't have household help—they use daycare where the baby learns to speak the language of the nannies at the day-care establishment and not the language you speak at home. The baby picks up habits of the nannies which may not be the habits you are comfortable with. But you have no choice. You need daycare because you need the job; because you need the money.

Finding your feet in your work environment

A young mother returning to work after a year or two does not find it easy. You have been out of circulation for too long and everything has changed. It's a jungle out there with a changed work climate, new work systems, new software, new and younger workforce, while your colleagues have already moved on or been promoted.

Getting your job back in your old place of work would be the best thing possible because you can ease into changes in the work systems. But if you cannot get your old job back, you are back in the market and have to take whatever you can get, generally with a hefty pay cut, because they know from the timelines on your resume that you are a young mother desperate for a job. They know and do not like the fact that you will be taking a leave of absence every time your child falls ill, and as a universal rule, children fall ill often.

Once you find employment, depending on your degree of desperation, there are a whole lot of other problems you have to find solutions to—antagonism in the workplace, condescension, sabotage and too often to ignore, varying degrees of sexual harassment. There is nothing you can quite put your finger on but it is there all around you. You feel the pressure and if you do not get your systems in place, that pressure keeps growing.

And then there's the guilt.

Working mothers and guilt go hand in hand. Why that happens is obvious. No one raises an eyebrow if the father works. If he opts to stay home, eyebrows are raised and heads are shaken, or he is praised. His role is that of the bread earner. Her role is of the nurturer. Society, that cantankerous old judge, does not approve of nurturers working outside the home.

How can one blandly presume that stay-at-home moms are nurturers? The tensions that stay-at-home mothers go through are unbelievable. Chores pile up and they are constantly on the run. A stay-at-home mom is trapped in a mentally and physically challenging existence and she is exhausted by the end of the day. She cannot risk falling ill.

Poor parenting from stay-at-home moms is actually quite understandable. There's no quality time for them unlike working moms, who can have quality time with the family. Even if they slip up occasionally or often, the working mom has the financial clout to demand that the family rally around.

Society is ready to sneer at how poorly you may perform in the office space and at home. If you are a working mom, society wants you to be the superwoman at work and at home. It would be great if society took over half your chores or even lent you a helping hand... but society is not at all concerned about helping you.

Instead, you find a good daycare for your baby, or your mother moves in with you and you can now apply for a job.

The working man has testicles and time. He can kickstart embryos but he doesn't grow them. He can work double shifts with no problem at all because he has his wife and mother or mother-in-law covering his ass at home. The working woman has no one covering her ass at home. Daycare may have taken the brunt of childcare during her office hours, but daycare comes with its own health challenges with runny-nosed kids in each other's faces, sharing love and germs equally. The working mom has to factor in at least one doctor's visit every fortnight.

Work smart, not hard

You are aware that you have taken a pay cut and you have to start proving yourself. Do you know what a corporate queen who made it big in business says? She says if you work smart, you *can* make it work for you. She says it's smart to learn the ropes of your seniors' jobs, but it is even smarter to learn your juniors' jobs because often, they are the ones who sabotage you.

Her diktat to all professional women is to build contacts in the chain of command going all the way to the top. Sleeping your way to the top is an urban myth, she says. You need to use your intelligence and keep an eye out for opportunity.

She says if you want to climb, study your workplace systems; there is always tweak room for efficiency. Put forward your suggestions only when the decision-makers are around, and make it sound like you just thought of it, from something they said.

She cautions that one must never confide in a colleague, a junior or one's immediate senior because they steal ideas. The trick is to do your job so well that your work is recognised by your seniors and by the competition too.

Make yourself indispensable at your place of work and network with the competition. You can still be given the boot by your employer if they can get someone half your age to work at half your wage, but you lose nothing by honing your skills. If you have networked well, your company's competitors will grab you to learn the secrets of your firm.

Own your own space at work too

You get that by mastering the job. It's not easy. Nothing is easy for women. You will have male colleagues making sexist jokes and talking down to you. They will hit you with that glass ceiling every time but you need to recognise that and just power through it. Sort out your work problems at work because you gain nothing by taking your work tensions home with you.

This applies to the first hint of sexual harassment too. Keep your Bullshit Radar on full alert and you can nip sexual harassment in the bud, by showing the perv that you do not have the time or inclination for this shit. Show the perv that you are not afraid to publicly call him out on it.

One of the most effective weapons we have today is a recording device. Keep your mobile phone with its video-taking ability easily available to record this confrontation. When you have downloaded it and saved it in several places, inform the perv that you will lodge a complaint with the authorities with recorded evidence. Do not ever back down from sexual harassment.

You have to be a taker at your workplace, not a giver. A taker on the work floor can afford to give every once in a while and it is immediately noticed and appreciated. A giver cannot take, ever.

No office romances. They serve no purpose, especially if one or both are married. It will end with one or both of you getting sacked. Let nothing come in the way of your limited time in your home with your family.

Set up systems at home

At home forgotten unimportant chores pile up and overwhelm you. The solution is to set up systems at home with clearly defined chores that have to be shared by all—husband, children and grandparents too. It doesn't have to be a Nazi-style regimen here—leave enough time for fun and enough flexibility to see that life is not a drag for any of you. Like your systems at the workplace, home systems too can be tweaked as you go along. Use every housekeeping and culinary shortcut you can think of.

Your home and family should be your go-to place for relaxation and security. If there must be a battlefield in your world, let it be at your workplace. You can resign from your position at work and find another job. You can find another career too. You cannot resign from motherhood.

You are in that for the long haul, so turn that home into the haven you and your family deserve. Don't try to fit yourself in wherever you can; instead, do all you can to tailor your home and family to fit around you.

Equal pay for equal work may not be a guarantee in the workplace, but equality in the family must reign supreme when it comes to household-related chores. If everyone in the family is enjoying equal board and lodging, then it stands to reason that the chores must be shared equally too.

The working mother comes home and the house is in a mess. She has to tidy, clean, cook, launder and be a loving mother to a bunch of lazy kids. Then she has to be a passionate sex partner to a horny idiot who will not share the chores with her. That's not on.

You have to put your foot down, or you will turn into a cantankerous, bitter old viper when you are in your thirties. This is your life; you have got to make it count—unless you get fulfilment working your fingers to the weary bone, from morning through night.

The jury is out on whether being a homemaker is more fulfilling or being a working mother is what it's all about. Working moms like the extra money coming in and they like the interaction with other humans that are not bound to them by blood or marriage. They like dressing up and getting out of the house. But without doubt the draw is the extra money coming in. And then there are women who have chosen to work from home, thinking it will be easier. This last option is not an easy one because you need an iron will to make a success of pursuing a career from home.

Guilt is mandatory, but don't give in to it

At home or at work, do not allow guilt to harsh your mellow. All working mothers feel varying degrees of guilt. If you are doing all the heavy lifting because of a sense of guilt that you are out of the house for ten hours of the day, stop and regroup.

First of all, address your guilt. Figure out when and where you are supposedly failing your family. Sort that out first. Then lessen your workload in the office and in the house. You do it by delegating work at both places.

While you may want to be Superwoman, the truth is—and I cannot say this often enough—no one cares.

If you have children at home, get them used to sharing the chores along with you and your husband. It is a great service you are giving them actually, when you assign jobs to them and hold them accountable. Consider it training for life in the workplace and when they run their own households. Their spouses will kiss your feet. They must know that there are no free lunches and no free rides. Someone *has* to pick up the tab. If everyone does their job then that's the best thing, right?

Working from home

If your skills are such that you can work from home, remember that the time frittered away by the commute is replaced by the time frittered away by domestic distractions—doorbells, kids doing really fascinating things, chores to be completed, meals to be shopped for, prepared and served, favourite television programmes, favourite books to be read, music you love, pets to be loved. You have to be ruthless. You have to carve out a dedicated space and time in your home for your work station, even if it is just your laptop on the dining table.

A work-from-home mom in my neighbourhood finishes her urgent household chores in good time before she is ready to begin work. She relaxes for an hour, showers, changes into office wear and begins work at ten o'clock. She takes a short lunch break and works till four in the evening. She changes out of her office clothes, into shorts and a tee and the rest of the day is hers. She does not work on weekends. Weekends are for relaxation. Her spouse and children have their lists of chores to be done when they are back from work and school. It's all very doable, she says, because they pull together.

6

Dealing with Your Snot-Nosed Adolescents

Did you think parenting was easy? Are your teenagers a nightmare most days? Do you practice what you preach? Do you think your kids can do no wrong? Do you have problems communicating with your teenagers?

You feel such a surge of love for your children as you watch them grow. You tell yourself that this is godliness that only a mother can feel. You have created a human or a couple of humans, maybe more if you love punishment and you are now raising them. You nurture them, you watch them grow and it's all good.

You see their guileless wide-open toddler eyes light up when they look at you. This is love, you conclude with deep delight.

Then again, it could it be only a feeling of great satisfaction that all in all you've done a pretty good job raising them. Personally, I say the light in their eyes actually means, 'Ah, this is our slave in whom we are well pleased'.

Some mothers are cook, maid and ATM rolled into one

It would be unwise to forget Rule Number One: children are not angels. They are small humans. They learn how to manipulate from the time they can open their little eyes. As they grow older, you will notice a perceptible shift in their priorities. As teens, they never stop watching you and they pick out your weaknesses and use them. No longer are you someone they are slightly nervous about. They are learning a lot and there are times when they will know some bits of trivia that you don't. That gets them all cocky but adds to the distance they are now mentally putting between themselves and you.

You will be faced with the Friends Situation. They feel embarrassed to introduce you to their friends. They do not encourage any conversation between you and their friends. Secrecy is the name of the game and you cannot question them. If you do attempt to do so, the tantrums begin.

Even worse is the silence, as they refuse to speak to you for daring to question them and 'embarrassing' them in front of their friends. At this time there is sullenness and no eye contact.

And because you love them so much, you accept it all, forgive all. They know what they want. They want freedom and the means to enjoy it. They come to you all smiling and cheery like butter wouldn't melt in their smarmy little mouths, asking you for cash or the use of your credit card. And you give it to them, because that's what you do. You need to be needed. They know this, because they have been observing you from birth.

They don't want to talk to you anymore. More importantly, they don't want you to talk to them anymore. Your brief as far as they are concerned is to provide them with a clean house, clean clothes, good food and cash on call.

If you are a mother who loves her children desperately, whose day begins and ends with them, you find as far as your adolescents are concerned, you are nothing more than a housemaid, cook and ATM rolled into one. And you accept that because you love them. And they take shameless advantage of you. And you know that too.

Taking the line of least resistance helps no one

The unfortunate thing in all this is that most parents take the line of least resistance. They don't want a scene because a scene is very stressful. It hurts them and somehow the reality of a scene makes them feel that they have failed as parents. As if to underline that feeling, their child tells them so.

You know it will be parental hara-kiri if you put your foot down. You watch that sweet innocent face you suckled at your breast not so long ago harden into Mein Fuhreresque lines. The thunderous scowl settles into cold contempt for you. You become a subnormal creature, someone whose job is to administer instant gratification to the crown prince or princess. And now? Now you are NOT doing your job! You are not doing what you are supposed to and you will suffer for that.

The lip curls into a sneer. Words come out, slowly at first, then in a rush. You hear that you are mean and hateful and that the little snot wishes you were dead. Do you feel that giant fist closing over your heart and squeezing the life out of you? That is a fairly accurate sign that *desperate* love for your child only gets you fucked.

What follows then is standard practice in most homes. You retire hurt; the little snot disappears into self-imposed exile to sulk in style. Next step, the deep freeze begins. You try to reason with your teen, you try to coax him into a good mood, you cook all his favourite foods and you finally give up and give in.

This time it is delayed gratification for the teen but he has won the war. Never again will you put your foot down; you won't have a leg to stand on, because the little snot has cut the ground out from under you.

When the little snot is a girl, you will find that girls can be even more calculating in their handling of a recalcitrant parent. They say girls are born wise. I call it born cunning. Like the Sphinx, you cannot really read what is going on behind that calm brow and that pretty gaze. Girls are all sugar and spice. They know exactly what they want and the way they get it is a chess grandmaster's delight. Their moves are planned at least twenty steps ahead of you. If you haven't laid down the golden rule that you are the boss when they cross six months, just give up quietly and go with the flow.

The girl knows how to soften you up, helping out just enough to delight you into congratulating yourself on having such a wonderful child. A good well-behaved child is a great advertisement for your parenting skills. You are a pillar of society.

Until you find that you've been patting yourself on the back so much you have twisted yourself tightly around her little finger.

After that, she will make you think that giving her what she wants is your heart's desire and not hers. Girls are very good at that. Until you cross her. A girl who is crossed can carry on a sulk fest to beat all sulk fests. It can go on for days, weeks, yes, even months. And need I say it? Okay, I'll say it. You are so screwed, you poor thing.

Never allow your child to treat you with contempt

Solution? You have to stop disrespect in its tracks when it is first directed at you. The child must know that he or she can disagree with your point of view, but on no account must they treat you with contempt. Stop it when it happens the first time. A cold hard look followed by a cold hard conversation is very effective.

Words delivered properly and promptly are way more effective than punitive action. Punishment makes both of you feel awful. Tell your child that you are the parent. Your job is not to be their friend. You love them and you will always love them; you will always have their back, but your job is to get them ready for life in the real world. And that is why you will not tolerate disrespect.

Use hard-clipped tones to inform the teenager that there are no free lunches because someone has to pay the bill. Both parents must be present and support each other in this confrontation. It never fails to work. With both parents in full steam, hell, the little snot dries up in a jiffy and toes the line in double-quick time, shaken and thoroughly stirred.

Or not.

There's the hard-boiled teen who could hear you both out and then say, 'I didn't ask to be born.' Here you will have to use common sense liberally. The common-sense answer would be a succinct, 'Well, you are here, so you have a choice. Do you want to behave sensibly, or do you want to behave like a twit?'

Never show fear. Never display wavering when dealing with a tantrum, or even a sulk. Kids are like animals in the jungle, waiting to see the fear or uncertainty in your eyes and body language.

You have to think on your feet. Every crisis will need different treatment. You don't want to turn the kid into a basket case, but you don't want the kid to turn into a self-obsessed adult either. A parent has to be a confessor, a judge, Mother Teresa and Attila the Hun when the situation demands it.

It's difficult but learn to admit your mistakes

A parent has to admit to parental mistakes too when necessary, because believe me, you will make many. And God, they are difficult to admit to. But with all this, before, during and after the battle, let the kids know that they can come to you for anything because you will always have their backs. If they know that and they know it without a doubt, you can do no wrong as a parent. Your big and small parental goof-ups will amount to nothing if your kids know that your love and support is unconditional.

Family and society will make excuses for murderers, thieves, terrorists, white-collar criminals, but God help you if you are a bad mother. That is the worst crime of all. When in doubt about your parental success or otherwise, remember this: you need to congratulate yourself for several achievements.

First, that kid can stand straight and glare at you. That means the kid is healthy—so you have met proper nutrition goals. Second, that kid is reading you the riot act—it takes confidence to do that and you have given that kid confidence. Third, that kid is unafraid of calling it out against authority—that's the best way to go through life.

Meanwhile, give that kid hell for disrespecting you; read him or her, the riot act. Do not give in. You can give in later, days later or a month later but for the moment be mad at them. Give no quarter for disrespect. Not your children, not your spouse, not your colleagues, not the random person on the street. Take no prisoners when it comes to disrespect aimed at you.

7

The Grandparents

You moved out of your parents' home but now your parents or in-laws have moved in with you. Is it annoying having them underfoot all the time? Are they cramping your style? Do they side with your kids ALL the time?

They flashed the sacrifices and money-spent-on-you cards during your formative years, time and time again. But now you have been through your own sacrifices and money-spending and you are waving the same cards at your own kids. Your parents realise that those won't work on you anymore so they try other tactics.

I'm not talking of those rare parents who prefer doing their own thing and who celebrate after the annual visit their kids and grandkids pay them is done and dusted. Those parents know what's what. It's the other parents I am talking about, who want to continue controlling their children and their grandchildren, who live vicariously through their progeny.

They pull the loneliness card from their stacked deck. They can manage to make themselves frail and vulnerable yet so full of dignity and grace. They tell you they are afraid of being alone. Not just of burglars breaking down their front door and murdering them to get their small bits and pieces of treasures gathered over the decades. They are afraid of illness, of paralytic strokes that will strike them down before they can even reach the telephone.

'Why, just the other day, Mum tripped when she was coming out of the bathroom. Lucky I was there to catch her, else who knows what might have happened... ' your father's hesitant voice peters out.

Mum will speak in halting accents of how Dad finds it difficult to climb up the ladder to fix the roof. How she's so afraid when he *still* insists on doing the odd jobs himself. He thinks he's still the strong Dad who used to swing you children up on his shoulder and build you doll houses and fix your toys.

They want one of two things: for you to move in with your spouse and children into their home or for them to move into your home with your spouse and children. You confabulate with said spouse.

Of course, the kids know they can milk their grandparents for treats and cash gifts beyond their wildest dreams. They want the grandparents in the house. Also, they know that without fail the grandparents will always take their side in any domestic spat and that you and your spouse will have to toe the line.

The average grandparents are grandkids' best friends forever. It is the natural order of life. Don't fight it.

Said spouse would be as big a pushover as you, why else did you guys marry? You agree to an elastic house, and the nightmare begins. Your parents start moving things around to make it easier for them to move around. They change your schedule to fit theirs. They spoil the children. This spoiling is of immediate and long-term strategic importance for them. They are building allies, cementing ties and fermenting rebellion.

Worse, grandparents get historical and grandchildren hang on to every slanderous word. The little snots cannot remember simple dates for their history test, but oh yes, they know which year you broke your leg, cycling down a hill on a bicycle with no brakes. They know when you went out on a date for the first time. They learn about all your dates and all your unrequited crushes. They learn all the tragedies in your life. They ignore the triumphs. They are hungry for more scandal, and your parents oblige with relish. And there you are feeding and housing the traitors.

This brings us to the money part of the new reality. While your parents seem to have an unending supply of cash to hand out to your kids, nothing much seems to be coming from them to share in the household expenses. Your food bill alone has increased by 50 percent, even though they eat minuscule amounts. You learn that your mother or father likes cooking up a storm for the grandchildren. The kids start looking plump but your wallet does not.

You have no privacy anymore. They are all over the house. Your sex life is shot to pieces because you never know when that gentle knock will come on the bedroom door. Sometimes they forget to knock. Also, the walls of modern houses are thin. Sex becomes a hurried, furtive affair, and when sex gets difficult at least one of you is going to get edgy and short-tempered.

Worse is how they treat your friends who visit. They 'accidentally' walk into the room while you are entertaining, linger around to be introduced, then sit down and take over the evening. They dish out advice, ask embarrassing, searching, intrusive questions, then laugh off the embarrassment of your friends by saying, oh, they've been there, done that. Your friends are uncomfortable and don't visit for a long, long time.

You notice that your parents start bringing in their friends. Card parties start, and strange old women come in and try out new recipes in your kitchen using your ingredients.

You cannot remonstrate with your parents. They have all the cards in their wrinkled old hands. You know you'll end up the joker in the pack if you try to halt the tide of parental takeover of your home and family. You would reach the end of your tether and think cunningly of ways and means of splitting the rebels. That would be a mistake.

Grandparents and grandchildren occupying the same war strategy room are like soldiers in a battlefield, supportive and protective of each other till the end. As mentioned before, it is part of the natural order of things and you don't want to disturb that.

Why don't you want to disturb that? Because, warts and all, grandparents make your life a little easier. They can be relied on to take care of the kids when you want to take off for a night on the town with or without your spouse. The kids are their natural allies and will go that extra mile not to distress the old biddies. You cannot put a price on that. An easy mind when you are out enjoying yourself or at work is a priceless treasure.

There's another purpose your parents and parents-in-law serve. Again, it is in the natural order for your parents to be highly critical of either you or your spouse or both. This brings the two of you closer together and you become natural allies against the onslaught of your immediate ancestors and descendants. Bottom line? It makes for a happier, warmer, merrier household.

That is until they get bedridden and you cannot afford private nurses round-the-clock. Then all family members are either busy or absent. It happened when you left the hospital with your newborn, and you discovered that you were left holding the baby. It will happen with your parents and you will be left holding the bedpan.

What can you do? The bottom line is you love your parents. They chose to give you life. They cleaned you, clothed you, fed you, put a roof over your head, educated you, nurtured you and loved you. Now it is your turn because that's the way the world turns. So you hold that bedpan, if you cannot pay for professional nursing help. The important thing to know is that this is a crisis that you and your parents can plan for because it can be managed smoothly. It is completely unlike that other one—the midlife crisis.

Part IV

Fly Over That Hill

1

The Adrenalin Rush of That Midlife Crisis

Did you think you were too old to fall in love? What will your family and friends say? Should you confess? Should you leave? You are sure you will be happy this time round. It's so exciting, falling in love again, right?

It happens to most people and it would be futile to fight it because a midlife crisis can be a lot of fun, provided you understand from the beginning that like a firecracker, it is bright, beautiful and burns out very quickly. The trick is to make sure you don't get burned and put at risk all that you hold dear.

This midlife crisis happens once your biological clock has stopped ticking and you are marking time to flatulence and a furry tongue. It hits both men and women. Recognise it as one last-ditch attempt to seize the day. It is one last opportunity to feel that glorious rush of romance, passion, intrigue and complete abandon. Regard it as a stab at adventure just one more time before you retire from the field.

Maybe it is something you have never done even at your most adventurous. Maybe you were too busy earning a living, building a family, making a life. Now you have done it all and you see the end of your life rushing at you like you're in an old car and the brakes don't work. There's so much you have not done. There's so much you did not dream you could do. And now suddenly it's there before you like a brand-new map to untold treasure.

It could be a beautiful sports car, or a man who makes you feel like a beautiful woman. The very best kind of midlife crisis would be one where the man treats you like a beautiful sports car.

If your midlife crisis is buying a flashy, powerful car, remember the seat belt, write your last will and testament and enjoy your machine. If it's a sexy man, make sure you don't make any hasty long-term commitment. The nature of a midlife crisis is that it's going to burn out before you know it and you don't want to be saddled with expensive baggage.

If it is someone of your own vintage, be very careful. It could be the start of something big and beautiful, or it could burn out and burn the both of you. I think it was Lord Byron who said, 'Love, like measles, is most dangerous when it comes late in life.'

The story of the Sap and the Yielding Widow

Midlife crisis completely messed up a gentleman of senior years, now known as the 'Sap' in his hometown. He was married to a nasty woman who bullied him, ridiculed him in public and kept control of his money. He met this quiet yielding widow and fell in love with her. Sap walked out of his house and down two roads to the yielding widow. His wife was enraged, then traumatised, then broken.

The entire neighbourhood was laughing at her, but they were also laughing at him. Sap told his wife to keep the house, the kids, the cars and the money. He wanted nothing, he said. He moved in with the yielding widow.

They were very happy for all of six months. Then they began having problems and the yielding widow stopped yielding. She advised him to return to his wife. He began visiting his bully wife and helping around the house. He found he was managing two households, one wife, one mistress and a gaggle of grown angry children.

His responsibilities increased. He was not happy. He was exhausted all the time. The bullying wife has resumed her bullying, because hey, no one changes. The mistress has now rented out her house and is living with her brother in another city. The Sap is back to square one and no one is speaking to him.

~

If both parties are unattached, it's no problem at all, but if both or one party is attached with all that baggage of spouse, children, in-laws, common friends and so on, then it's a whole stinking mess you would do well to steer clear of. It just isn't worth the pain. That's the kind of mess you do not want at *this* point in your life.

You have one of three options if you feel that powerful attraction:

- You can walk away and never have any intimate contact at all.
- You can both agree to continue the friendship bringing the two families together and something beautiful and platonic grows out of it, with just that delicious undercurrent of romance. This is exciting but difficult because it calls for great acting prowess of both parties.
- Have a rip-roaring affair, get it out of your system and never get caught. And never, *ever* confess to your spouse or to anyone else. This would be easier to handle, but it takes nerves of steel. It needs meticulous planning by the two concerned parties.

You will in all probability get caught eventually, but it's great while it lasts. It will be even greater to marvel over in your last years if you are not caught. Once you are caught, you are fucked. Worst-case scenario—you lose everything to the cheated spouse and you are a pariah to all your friends and family who love your spouse.

It doesn't work if you are thinking long-term

After the first heady rush of discovering mutual love and passion, the rest of the world crowds in, and you cannot help but realise that the shit is really going to hit the ceiling fan if you two go public with your love. Or get caught.

If you sit down and make a list of the number of close family and friends who will be hurt or distressed by your liaison you will, on average, find at least fifty people—friends, relatives, neighbours, colleagues, who will be hurt and who will lose all respect for you.

Once that realisation dawns, be aware that it's the beginning of the end. One or both of you will withdraw with the old clichés of 'It's not you, it's me' and 'I cannot hurt him/her' and 'I will never do anything to disrespect you'. It has to end and you are both so fucked. You have to pull out of the relationship because both of you are too old to deal with the fallout. It's painful but necessary.

Always remember that no matter what wild promises are made, neither of you will be willing to take the risk of hurting those closest to you. Accept that this will not last, because it cannot last. Guilt has a way of taking the fun out of a secret romance.

There's another reason why it does not work out in so many cases. If you do happen to burn your bridges, leave your respective spouses, children, families and set up a life for yourselves when you are both in your fifties or sixties, you will have all and *more* of the adjustment problems of a young couple starting out.

Adjusting in old age is no fun at all. Once you cross fifty, you are set in your ways. As in the first flush of young love, you naturally project all that is good and loveable about yourself. So does your opposite number. Remember you did the exact same thing when you were young. But the difference between you today and you as part of a young couple is that young couples can make adjustments, even radical adjustments, but older couples cannot.

There will be farting under the covers and roof-rattling snoring. There will be drool on the pillows. There will be picking up after the slob, male or female. There will be different types of music, food, and entertainment that each will want to prioritise.

There will be friends who will anyway look at the other woman or man with distrust, even dislike, because they would have known the original spouse for many years. Some close friends will even drop out of your life. Others will treat you like an outcast in case what you have is contagious and their spouses might catch it.

Sometimes sadness laced with regret sets in and that's the worst situation to be in. Hiding, intrigue and secrecy were the best parts of the midlife crisis, but now that you have both taken the plunge, what you are left with is an ordinary relationship between a man and a woman.

Chores still have to be done. Bills still have to be paid. The sex wasn't all that great to start with and you find you have exchanged only one part of your earlier equation. The problem remains the same. If your marriage did not work out the first time around, remember, you were one half of that failed marriage and you carry that one half into the new relationship.

If love has to come late in life, let it be between two unattached friends. Not between two attached ones.

Now if both are attached and both agree that this will be a no-strings attached affair that will die a natural death, you could have the time of your life, provided, I stress again, you don't get caught. Also provided that you don't find yourself covered in guilt and have to make the Grand Confession. Never make the grand confession.

The grand confession only makes bad worse. Keep your indiscretions to yourself because there is no point served in spreading misery. If there are suspicions and you are accused, lie and lie again. You will feel guilt, but that's the price you have to pay for that one brief adventure when you flew so close to the sun and survived. Anyway, guilt is good for the soul.

There's also a very human feeling of delicious triumph that is all to the good since the midlife crisis generally hits during menopause, which is far from a bad thing if you make menopause work for you.

2

Make Menopause Work for You

Are you dreading menopause? Do you try your best to hide your hot flashes and mood swings? Is sex painful? Do you feel less of a woman? Do you feel dowdy and old? Do you think life as you know it is over?

Menopause is that time of life women dread. Women hitting menopause presume wrongly that this is the end of life for them. They are quite wrong. If you open your eyes and read the fine print Nature gives you on a platter, menopause is the best thing to happen to you. It's the time you allow yourself to pause and reflect and make a good plan for the immediate future. Menopause is Nature's sign to women to reclaim their lives.

The public perception about menopausal women is that they have mood swings and are prone to hot flashes, that they suffer from aches and pains and are broody. Use that, because the truth is many women have no such symptoms.

Yet whether you have them or you don't, you would be foolish not to use that knowledge and let your family know that they should expect mood swings from you. Explain to them what hot flashes are. Set your scene.

Whether you are menopausal or not, many are the times when you have been so stressed out, so annoyed, so irritated by the actions and inaction of your family members that you wanted to hit someone hard. Yet you found it was easier to swallow your spleen and pick up after them.

You had no free time to speak of then, but now look around you. The members of your family are all grown up and grown old. But you are still picking up after them. Stop doing that. This is your time.

Take back your life. Find that spark that you know you have and give it life. Find a hobby, or find a number of hobbies, get new clothes with accessories, call up friends, go out and meet them. Go for a drive. Travel. Take in a movie, have high tea, damn, go clubbing too. Just take back your life.

This is the time when your oestrogen, like your children, packs up and leaves. It is the hormone that supposedly makes you feminine. That's ridiculous! Once you stop menstruating do you turn into a man? I don't see no penis sprouting. Your vagina dries and your menstrual periods stop. I don't know about you, but I longed for menopause like a dog for a bone.

Menstruation is nasty. You get cramps, you feel smelly, you bleed for a week, month after bloody month. You cannot put a pressure bandage on it and lie down. No, you have to continue life as though it's just another day on the factory floor.

Imagine an entire week of being aware of a sometimes continuous, sometimes intermittent flow of blood out through your vagina of all places. You live in hourly fear of staining your clothes if it is a heavy-flow day. You are worried about body odour; you are worried about chafing and blisters. That's eighty-four days in a year.

You have been bleeding for a total of almost three months of the year, every year from the age of nine or ten or eleven or twelve right up until fifty. How many years is that? And they call us the weaker sex.

Now it stops. You are wonderfully dry and you are without cramps. You are fragrant. You are free. What's not to love about menopause? Yes, the hot flashes and mood swings are no picnic, but they can be sorted out with a little help. You also get used to them and hey, just *see* the possibilities when you can use them to your own advantage.

With menopause, hygiene becomes the easiest thing, sex becomes painful, but you know that there are various lubricants that can be used. If you don't want the hassle of going to a doctor and getting a prescription for a vaginal cream, reach for good old pure coconut oil or petroleum jelly and use that as a vaginal lubricant. There is also that whole hormone replacement therapy available, but check with your doctor about the possible side effects like breast cancer.

The very best part of menopause is that it gives you a psychological advantage over the entire male and young world. The fear of pregnancy is over and out. The necessity to fake orgasms is out. Don't deny that you faked orgasms when all you wanted was to just sleep. Faking hot flashes is easy.

Just grab a fan and a towel; fan yourself furiously and mop your face. You can have mood swings without holding back because by now the kids are grown and mood swings are a good way to keep your spouse in the house on his toes. Mood swings are easy too and take it from me, they are very liberating.

Mood swings, if used intelligently, can turn a doormat into a flying carpet. You have been the obliging, sweet woman, loving wife and patient mother all these years when what you really felt like doing was to reach for the cleaver. Now you can get into a full-blown foul mood, say what you want, do what you want, and refuse to do anything you don't feel like doing.

You can say your piece softly, which is more menacing, or you can scream it out loud, which is more satisfying. After the man has been shaken and stirred, you can come down from your mood and blame it on menopause. After that, be as sweet as you can be, ply him with goodies, sweetness and delight. The moment you are thwarted, fly into the high fidgets again. Make menopause work for you.

This is your time. Do not waste it. The kids are grown, and if you are married to a man who has taken you for granted all your married life, then this, my friend, is the time for you to give back as good as you got. If your grown kids are still living under your roof, you can get them in line too, not just the spouse.

Give them hell, then contritely blame it on the hot flashes and be extra sweet to them. Then give them hell again the next time they put a foot wrong. Take back your space. Nature has given you a practical instrument, so use it. Ask your doctor about a good working diet, vitamin B12, calcium and oestrogen supplements, and then just enjoy yourself. Don't fritter away your menopause. It's a frigging gift.

The only thing that is stupid about menopause is the weight gain and the boobs. Your breasts become gigantic and not in a good way. The left one wants to move to the left and sag while the right one slides to the right and sags. Give yourself a treat. Join a gym and get a professional to help you use the right exercises in the right manner.

It sorts out two problems. Your boobs reduce along with the fat in the rest of your body and your bones get strong, so osteoporosis doesn't break your hip while you are taking a stroll. Apparently, you don't fall and break your hip. Your hip bone breaks because it is so porous and weak and the fracture causes you to fall. So get a good exercise regimen going and you're set.

Notice how some women look better than they ever did during menopause? They own their space, walk with grace and they command respect. They look good, they dress elegantly or wildly, but they are comfortable in their skin. It merely needs a bit of physical and mental exercise.

Like infancy and adolescence, menopause is just another stage in your life, but this is the stage where you command the spotlight. I've been through the stages, but this one, menopause has the most going for it. Freedom, is what I call it. Turns out, this is the time your kids also leave to start their own lives and you are left with the empty-nest syndrome. Here too you have a choice: drown in sorrow or grow wings.

3

An Empty Nest Means You Can Spread Your Wings

Are you missing your children to the point of misery? Do you long to hear their voices in the next room instead of through the phone? Do you miss looking after them? Does the day just stretch endlessly?

It's that time of life when your children leave home for higher studies or to get a job outside your state or country. It is more traumatic for the mother who had given every waking hour to raising and nurturing her children. The mother who drove them here and there, picked up the slack, sat up with them the whole night through when they were ill or working on school and college projects, sent them to bed and sat through till dawn sticking pictures and colouring in their projects so they would be rested for the next day, and loved their friends and hated their enemies... that mother gets hit solidly.

If you are that mother who put her own life on hold to make sure her children had her idea of the perfect life, then you will suffer from empty-nest syndrome more severely than the other mother who had a job of her own or maybe ran her own business, big or small.

After my kids moved out of the state for higher studies, I did strange things. I would pad around the house heavy-hearted and pick fights with the spouse. I gave full focus to being miserable. Not only would I listen for their voices, I would even imagine hearing their voices and just be a perfect pain. Like some wild animal I would open their wardrobe and take a deep breath, inhaling their scent from the clothes they had left behind.

I would lie on their beds, until I realised two things: they were never coming back and I was turning into a basketcase. After completing their academics, they would get jobs and after getting jobs, they would marry or set up their own households and I would never have them under my roof permanently again.

It was a lonely, helpless feeling. One needs a peg—no, not a peg of booze, a peg to hang the sadness up to dry. I found my peg in music.

While fiddling with their stuff, I stumbled on their boombox and discovered a twenty-four-hour radio channel that broadcast my type of rock music. The first song was an Iron Maiden one and I took it as a sign. The music played after that from morning till night, soothing, entertaining, lifting the sadness. I could focus on doing other things. I began a small online op-ed type of enterprise, which did surprisingly well. I was sorted.

It also helped that once my kids got their jobs and their spouses, they completely forgot about me. I had to call the little snots. I had to keep the lines of communication open. Letting grown children move into the 'uncaring zone' is not advisable.

Keep them engaged and current on your status quo so they cannot remain uncaring. You need to keep the bonds strong because when they need help in a crisis, it is going to be difficult moving out of your comfort zone to help an uncaring kid.

So what do you do when you have to rattle around in a silent childless house? You can do lots of shit.

The empty-nest time is the best time to focus on your own life, on your comfort, on maybe earning some extra money for yourself. Yes, you have saved and you have a good number of solid blue-chip investments, but there are few things as nice as getting fresh finance into your kitty that you can spend without a worry.

In this time of your life, therefore, you need three things: committed friends, some extra money that you can fritter away and something to do with your time.

There's no such thing as having 'too many' friends

The thing you must do is widen your circle of friends to include some who share your worldview and a few who do not. If you can manage it, include people of different cultures. Most of all, it is imperative that you make friends with people of all age groups from toddlers to nonagenarians.

Get out of the house. If the Covid-19 virus is still around when you are reading this, remember to wear a mask, keep at least a metre's distance from other people while you stop to chat with your neighbours. Short, breezy, hey-how-you-doing kind of thing. If they want a longer conversation, share one with them.

Oh, important point: get friendly with the thugs in the neighbourhood too and offer what help you can—they are the ones who will drop everything to help you when you ask for it.

Forget all the negatives you hear about social media. It's the best platform for you to meet people, provided you keep your private life out of it. The way to make social media work for you is to keep it light and easy. Don't buy into anything that is sold to you.

Join a few groups that share the same interests as you. Listen to different points of view while getting your own out there in a public forum. Avoid pouring your heart out in personal messages. Better still, avoid personal messages entirely. Stick to the post. Get interested in the world. The world has everything for you. It's the ultimate nest and it is never empty.

Social media commandment: If it's too good to be true, it's a lie

One rule in social media is to always remember if it is too good to be true, it is generally a lie. Don't get carried away by anyone, unless you know them in the real world and you know where they live, so you can send the cops to their house if they cheat you of your hard-earned savings. Don't fall for any hard-luck stories people pitch to you, or investment offers that are too good to be true.

One airhead who was suffering badly from empty-nest syndrome got onto social media and fell in love with a handsome man nine years her junior. His profile picture showed him to be a well-formed forty-five-year-old. All other photos on his profile page were memes. His profile details showed he was a consultant, looking for friendship and interested in single ladies. That was so cute, the airhead thought.

Their friendship blossomed unbelievably rapidly. She was in love. He told her he was very busy setting up his business in another part of the country. He was struggling to find that last tranche of funds to set up his office because his venture capitalist died. He was ready to pay an interest of 12 percent per annum.

She promised to lend him the money interest-free. She loved him, see? He refused of course, but she insisted. He sent her an account number. Her money was transferred. He continued chatting with her every night for exactly a month more and suddenly his social media account was closed. She had no telephone number and no address.

All she had were some great pictures of him that turned out to be fake. Finally, she went to the cops. They could not trace the social media account. The money she lent him had been withdrawn over the month and the bank account was now closed. The address furnished to the bank was a rented apartment waiting for a new tenant. He had all the hallmarks of a con artist, they said, one who preys on lonely women.

But if you have a bit of common sense, social media can rock your world in the nicest possible way. Take my Bird Lady who went out of her way to review each chapter of this book as I completed it. Here's how she handled her empty nest.

She got in touch with her school and college friends and

meets them regularly out of home. To keep her brain cells oiled, as she puts it, she joined an online riddling group where she made a load of wacky friends. People post a lot of photographs on social media, so she got interested in photography.

'Figured, if they can do it, why can't I?' She bought herself a beginner's DSLR, read all there was to read about photography on the Internet, began with flowers, then landscapes, then decided to do something more challenging and took up bird photography.

She met qualified bird photographers and picked their brains, then bought herself a better camera with a powerful zoom lens. She says, 'Now I jump at the chance of a trip, walk all over the place with my camera inviting curious stares and questions... silver-haired woman walking around the countryside with a big lens in her hand... I have become a curiosity for folks. Even when I visit my daughter, I pore over maps looking for birding spots.'

One series of photographs she took of a gripping fight to the finish between a rat snake and a juvenile eagle was published in a leading nature magazine. She made social media work for her.

Find an occupation that can earn you money you can fritter away

Find a part-time job; no matter if it is way below what your qualifications merit. Sign up for an occupation that will engage you, delight you and pay you for your effort. It could be anything. Look to your strengths, or do something completely new.

You can manufacture or you can be employed. Just do not let that occupation take up all of your time. A maximum of four hours is enough to devote to your revenue-earning model of whatever. If it doesn't work for you, change it. Write, or cook, or sew, or design, do carpentry, breed fish, or consult, or choose any occupation that you have the capacity for. Keep an eye out for that which engages you.

A retired accountant who was successful in her investments offered to help her share broker balance his accounts for a small remuneration. Since she was not officially on their payroll, she used her fee to buy and sell shares. She makes a tidy sum and takes off every six months to go on a cruise. Her most recent cruise was to the North Pole.

Who's to say that your kids won't bung you into an old-age home as soon as they can afford it and want you out of their house, or your own? Be warned, it's been known to happen. Do you know when it cannot happen? It cannot happen when you have an independent income. You can then bung yourself into a senior citizen luxury condo of your own choice.

Find something to do with your time

Menopause and the empty-nest syndrome most often happen at the same time. You have a shot at glorious freedom with both these conditions. With menopause, you are free of bloating, bleeding and cramping. With the empty nest, you are free of day-to-day tedious chores like waking the kids, fixing their meals, taking them shopping, sorting out their squabbles, following up on their academics, picking up after them, or doing their laundry. You are still responsible for them as long as you live but you don't have the *tedium* anymore. Celebrate that.

You have an empty nest. This means you literally have more room to spread your wings. There's all that extra space in ye olde family homestead. That's pure gold. Look at the kids' room or rooms and figure out what you can do with the extra space. You can turn the room into a bed-sitter and take in a paying guest or an exchange student so you will have another kid around to mother and play mind games with and earn a chunk of cash too.

If you don't want the responsibility of another young human being, then turn it into your sanctuary that can be converted back into a bedroom should the kid return. Yes, they often return to lick their wounds when the independence they so desperately fought for bites them in the ass.

You can turn it into a gym. Bring in an elliptical or a treadmill or just put in indoor flowering plants, some mats, incense and a giant wall-mounted TV screen and turn it into a meditation room. Pick up a new hobby—furniture restoration, writing or painting, anything that engages you. You can turn the walls of the room into your canvas and paint giant flowers or a delicate tracery of tiny things all over the walls and ceiling. Your choices are limitless.

Make full use of the menopausal mood swings and the empty-nest syndrome. If your husband or partner has ideas of turning that room into a den for himself, put your foot down and stake claim to the empty room. Part of the whole deal of getting older is that you get a stab at mental and physical peace once again. Why fritter away a chance at enjoying the years ahead?

You could also take a leaf out of the book of the pious widow in my neighbourhood. She found Religion and is fanatically happy about it. She goes around the block doing Good Deeds even when they are not requested or appreciated. People duck behind their drapes when they see her march down the street. She does charity and helps the local religious organisation make entries in their many registers. She is happy because she is sure when she pops off, she is going to meet her Maker and He will be well pleased with her. The point is she has found her bliss. Now you find yours.

This is your penultimate hurrah. The second last one. It will transition you into the rocking old age of your life. A rocking chair is optional.

4

Age Disgracefully and Rock That Rocking Chair

Do you want to fight against going quietly into the night? Are you afraid of making a fool of yourself? Do you think your friends and family will laugh at you? Do you agree that there will be enough time to sleep after death?

~

I believe in ageing disgracefully. Do what you want, experiment with your look, seek out like-minded friends. Avoid those that make you feel old and useless. Some people age faster than others. The ageing begins in their thoughts, their bodies follow obediently and then everything just deteriorates. Others are resigned to the prospect of old age and death, and you see them timorously taking maximum precautions hoping for a peaceful end.

A growing number of older people refuse to sink quietly into the night. At the risk of boring you, I repeat those titanium words: you have a choice. Every step of the way you have a choice. It is your mind that determines how soon the ageing kicks in.

People who will not go quietly into the night

Mr P is eighty years old. He has silver hair and a salt 'n pepper beard. He has a beaky nose, an explosive temper and a heart that is as soft as silk. He is an interior designer who loses more money than he earns and he earns big money. Does he care? He does not. It's the thrill of thinking up a project and seeing it through that pushes him. He is a potty-mouth who is adored by his friends and family.

Mr P sees mothers of disabled children sitting around gossiping while their kids are at a special school. He does not like seeing perfectly healthy people sitting around and doing nothing productive, so he asks them why they don't do something with their time. They say they know nothing apart from sewing, cooking and cleaning. He convinces them to sew. Sew dusters, make aprons, sell them, make money, do something with your time, he tells them.

He gets a fashion designer to give him a design for aprons. Those are to be sold at malls. They make dusters. He forms linkages between the institution in which their kids are being trained, gets second-hand sewing machines for the mothers—forty Brother sewing machines, no less. He gets a qualified tailoring instructor to teach them. And he gets buyers for their products. Finally they are working. They are thrilled to be earning money. Their neighbours want to join in too. He gets more sewing machines and an enterprise is born. And that's just one of the things he does. Sinking quietly into the night is just not his style.

Distinctly the reverse of his character is a woman I know who succumbs to her aches and pains of old age. She sits and does nothing. She moans and whines about everything that happens or does not happen to her. She is in and out of hospitals all the time, but never dies even though she claims to pray for death. She lives on to suffer a miserable existence and spread that misery around.

~

My second hero is Dame R. She deserves this title. Dame R is ninety-three years old and lives alone. She has a daily maid who comes in to do the rough work, but she cooks for herself, launders her own clothes, and tends to her garden. Passersby hear Dame R chuckling or laughing or cheering with her television set on at high volume—she loves watching sports, soaps, news, and religious and travel channels on television.

She had a fall a year back, and was bleeding profusely from a head injury. She managed to crawl to her front door to keep it open in case she passed out from blood loss when help arrived. Then she crawled to the telephone to call for help.

She was rushed to casualty where the doctor ran the usual tests and asked her the standard questions to test for concussion. Dame R dutifully answered, then grabbed his arm and told him urgently, 'Listen, Doctor! Make sure you shave off only a little hair around the wound. It's my grand-daughter's wedding in a week's time and I want my hair to look nice.' This has become the doctor's standard party story.

Hands down, Dame R is my benchmark for having a handle on ageing without getting old. Her mind is sharp and always engaged. It comes from a sturdy, healthy upbringing. She used to be an athlete in her youth, then married and settled down with her beloved husband and five children. She cuts her own hair in a Princess Diana style cut that was all the rage when Lady Di was alive and well. It still looks good though. She wears palazzos at home and uses a walking stick. She won't give up and go quietly into the night.

My third hero is Mr H, my school pal's dad. They lived in this lovely tile-roofed cottage in a narrow leafy lane in the suburbs. He made amazing architectural models that our teachers used as teaching tools quite often. I remember we were studying Japan and he made a traditional Japanese house with his magical fret saw and paint and paper and love. The curved roof, the doors, the paper walls with paintings on them, tatami mats, and the little tables for the tea ceremony were all pieces of perfection.

Mr H has always been slim as a reed and very tall. He once fell through an open sewer manhole, but his long arms instinctively flew out and he managed to hang there resting his elbows on the road, while his slender body dangled below, over the smelly sewer. All that could be seen of him was his head and shoulders emerging from the road and his arms taking the entire weight of his body. A man hove into sight, saw Mr H calmly hanging there and asked him what he was doing. Mr H snapped that he was taking the air and then told him to 'stop asking stupid questions and go get help.' He got help and Mr H lived to tell the tale.

I visited my old school pal and she yelled out to her dad to come and see who had dropped by. He walked in his usual graceful manner, eyes clear, no spectacles, no walking stick, only stooping slightly. We talked and we talked. The years gone by were nothing. Adventures of school were unwrapped from the distant past and marvelled over. I noticed the roof of their pretty little cottage was covered with tarpaulin. A massive rain storm was due to hit in two days. I asked him if his roof leaked.

'This year's not too bad,' he said, 'because we've covered it with a tarp. It looks ugly, but I can't climb up on the roof and replace the broken tiles.'

'Of course, you cannot...' I said.

'I'm too old now. I did it every year, right until I was ninety. Now? Forget it!'

'Till... until... until you were nin...! How old are you now?'

'Ninety-three. I'm not climbing on that damn roof.'

~

Don't give up your old pastimes. If you cannot physically manage some of them, find new hobbies, connect with people of your own age, yes, but definitely people who are younger than you too.

Take your age factor out of your dealings with people. In

your mind you are twenty-one, the year you were ready to take on the world. No one thinks of death and disease at twenty-one; neither should you at ninety-one. Just go with the flow. If you drop dead, hey, at least you used up all your minutes and you owned your space.

Do not depend on your children

If you notice, I have not factored your children into being around you and holding your hand, being your eyes and your legs. I have not mentioned the possibility of your children rushing to help you with your chores and shopping. Because while some children do that, most don't, you know? Not because some of them are ungrateful cretins—many are struggling with their own lives. My schoolmate is an exception to the rule. Actually, my generation is an exception to that rule. My peers did drop everything to look after their ailing parents. They were wired differently.

So many of today's adult sons and daughters are trying to keep their shit together and don't seem to be managing too well. They have all the gadgets, all the scheduling, all the time-saving mechanisms of today's tech marvels, yet Life has become too complicated for them. They are struggling to keep their sanity. You could sort out their problems for them for free, but they prefer visiting their shrink more often than they visit you. Therefore, your children may not be able to be around when you need them. Accept that as a fact of life.

You can tell whether they will rally around you, or whether they will be loving from afar. Or conspicuous by their absence when you are down and out, ill or just lonely when you are in your 50s and 60s. It's the little things you have to take note of. They are a sign of things to come.

Pay careful attention to how your sons and daughters treat you. If there is any frequent talking down to you when you cross sixty, be on your guard. If there is continuous impatience with your point of view, accept that they think you are a nuisance. If there is condescension for whatever you do, or a complete lack of interest in whatever you undertake, take careful note. If you fall ill or get a slight injury, see if they show any signs of worry or care. If they don't, that's your sign. Start making plans to hire help for when you are old. You cannot rely on them to help you when you need it.

If those children of yours are not good to you when you are hale and hearty, they will be no good for you when you are weak and ailing. They will use you for grandparenting duties but once the grandkids reach school age, your services are pretty much dispensed with. Then you won't merely feel lonely and useless, you are going to be resentful too. So do the smart thing: focus on doing what you love and make contingency plans for old age early on in life.

If you get along well with your kids, great, but their spouses and their kids are not really flesh of your flesh and bone of your bone. Just one misunderstanding is enough to set a whole shitload of similar misunderstandings in motion, so step back. Give them space. Concentrate on your own space. Get on with your own life. If they are close and loving, count yourself lucky.

Just make sure you have sufficient investments earning you a decent income, good medical insurance, or, if you are so inclined, leave a signed DNR (Do Not Resuscitate), which means no use of CPR if your heart stops beating, and a working plan for enjoying your life doing what you love to do. It could be anything, building model planes, finding a cure for cancer, needlepoint, or just the pure joy of doing absolutely nothing.

This is your last lap. Do you want to fade away, or do you refuse to give up on life? Sure, the average older woman will have limitations on how much she can do physically, though there are women burning up social media with videos of dancing, weightlifting, hiking, racing, cycling, painting, writing, helping others. Pamper yourself, dress up occasionally or often and give yourself frequent treats.

Spend a bit on personal grooming. Hair styling, manicures, pedicures, massages. Doing your own toes is a bitch, if you cannot bend properly. They say there is grace and elegance in ageing and that one should age gracefully. You can if you wish, but where's the joy in that?

There is joy in ageing disgracefully. So colour your hair if you wish, wear bright clothes, buy into the latest fads that you like, listen to loud music, dance—just have fun. In the game of life, you have reached the rocking-chair level. See that you ace it. Rock that rocking chair. Do not go gently into the night.

Put the fun into your funeral

There's one thing I must add. No, not your last will and testament. That is up to you, if you want to do it. Kind, sensible parents will make a will so their children don't fall out or have to chase banks to claim your doubloons. If your children don't give a damn about you, then every instinct of mine rebels against you making a will if you are a neglected parent. Keep your affairs in order.

Keep your investments neatly listed, your property titles clear, and your moolah clearly inventoried. If you have a lot of wealth to leave your children, let them do the running around after you pop off. Why should they get their greasy little paws on your savings and investments over the decades without putting in any effort? Let them work for it.

If you have nothing much to leave for them, no point in making a last will and testament, right? But there is one thing you must, absolutely must do. You must plan your own funeral.

Put the fun back in funeral.

I plan to print open-ended invitation cards to my funeral. I want to be cremated. Yes, there can be a church service, but I stopped being pious three decades ago, and I seriously doubt I'll find religion any time soon. So okay, a church service if they want to have one followed by my cremation. The church service is optional; the cremation is mandatory.

My ashes can be placed in any receptacle, a brown paper bag would be ideal. I will keep money aside for a wild party on board a river cruise boat for my friends and family with my ashes to be poured into the river in the neighbourhood, before dinner. Everyone may be too drunk after dinner.

Why the river? Because I have always loved travelling and the river will carry my ashes far and wide. What's not to love? I will go where the river takes me. I'm not picky; I'll take the rough with the smooth, the way I always have. I hope you do too. Make every minute count. It's the only way to be.

So I take my leave; hopefully I have covered as much as it is possible to cover in the life of the twenty-first century woman. I'll probably be dead by the time this treatise is published, but if you have read through the chapters and not just the last one, my work here is done. Listen to this old woman who's wise and *knows* her shit. Follow your bliss.

Acknowledgements

If you are writing a book, you need someone to nag you to write it. That someone was Sharon Fernandes, who died young two Christmases ago and broke my heart when this book was only half done. Then came other friends who are published authors: Gautam Benegal and Wendell Rodricks, who liked the first chapter and cheered me on and even promised to help me find a publisher.

Not only did Wendell promise to make sure my ashes would be immersed in the river after I pop off, he promised to launch this book of mine. Yeah. He died just before Covid-19 hit and left a hollow space in me that hurts every so often.

Then ace amateur bird photographer Mamta Kacker Muttreja, a no-nonsense academic, asked to read my book. She is my Book Whisperer. Despite birding-related photography trips all over the place, Mamta read the chapter the day I emailed her. That chapter was put to bed only once she replied either 'Love it!' or 'Wow'.

Vikram Batra took offence at the beginning of the book, twenty-one drafts ago, then he read it again and told me to ignore what he said and to get this book published because it will save lives.

My deep gratitude to Computer Whisperer and musician Rajeev Kumar aka Lunarwolf, who helped me recover and clean the corrupted file of my manuscript.

Once it was done, Ash Nallawalla edited the manuscript and gave me valuable inputs that got me rewriting the manuscript twenty-one times until I was happy with it.

Thanks also to Abbas Bagasrawala who took the time to do deep editing of one chapter and instructed me to tag men to read this book too.

I will always be indebted to Nishi Malhotra for connecting me to literary agent Kanishka Gupta of Writer's Side Literary Agency, who, within a couple of days, said he and his editor loved the book and would find a good publisher for it. Celebrated authors Shobhaa De and Wendell Rodricks blew me away by writing the nicest blurbs for my book.

Thanks to Sucheta Potnis, Snehalata Naidu, Minakshi Batra and Bharathi Shenoy who gave me the encouragement to continue, wishing that they had had this book to guide them through the milestones of life. A big thank-you to old school friend Mira Shah, who edited the last chapter without being asked. A special shout-out to Nina Chandi who grinned here and there when she read the teens chapters and told me seriously, 'Bevinda Aunty, this book must be translated into all the regional languages of India.'

And last but not least my sister Maria Vitoria Dias, a Grammar Nazi of the worst kind who read two chapters, approved of the idea but not what she called foul language and told me that I would get a publisher for my book, never fear, because this book was meant to be read.

My deepest thanks to all those who have cheered me on. That you are in my life proves that I must have done something right. This book is like my child and I see that it takes a village to raise this child too.

My gratitude to world-famous mental health professionals who, thanks to YouTube lectures and interviews, helped corroborate my views on so many ticklish relationship issues. They have most generously allowed me via email to quote them in this book where required. They are: Pamela Meyer, author of *Liespotting;* Adam Lodolce, author of *Men Love Confident Women*; David A. Sbarra, PhD professor, Department of Psychology, University of Arizona, also president, Academy of Psychological Clinical Science; Leslie Morgan Steiner, author of memoir, *Crazy Love;* Dr Ramani Durvasula, clinical psychologist, author of *Should I Stay or Should I Go: Surviving A Relationship with a Narcissist* and Bernardo Villafañe, clinical social work/therapist, LCSW, in his video on *Domestic Violence* and psychologist Guy Winch, author of *How to Fix A Broken Heart.*

I have also quoted a few other international professionals from their open source video presentations and lectures: authors David Maxfield and Joseph Grenny a.k.a. The Behavioural Science Guys in their YouTube video *One Simple Skill To Overcome Peer Pressure*; Dr Zhana Vrangelova, PhD in Developmental Psychology from Cornell University in her TEDx talk, *Is Casual Sex Bad For You?* and Jane Epstein, nurse practitioner specialising in adolescent medicine, in her TEDx talk *Why We*

Need To Talk To Girls About Sex. Finally a solemn doffing of the hat to the editors associated with the publisher Amaryllis, Rashmi Menon, managing editor, and Archana Ramachandran, editor, who gave valuable inputs and ruthlessly removed a few out-of-the-box ideas I had offered to keep adolescents shaken and stirred, like a video of their arrival into this world.

If you are still reading this, then thank you too, dear reader. Please gift this one and get another one for yourself. I need this book to be read not just in India but across the world. The compatibility quiz could prevent poor relationships and the chapter on domestic violence could save lives. The rest of it, even if I say so, is quite an excellent blueprint for today's woman to help set tomorrow's woman on her feet.

www.ingramcontent.com/pod-product-compliance
Lightning Source LLC
La Vergne TN
LVHW100524110826
845146LV00002B/770

* 9 7 8 9 3 9 0 9 2 4 7 6 9 *